JOB:

Poet of Existence

JOB:
Poet of Existence

by Samuel Terrien

THE BOBBS-MERRILL COMPANY, INC.

Indianapolis   New York

The following permissions are acknowledged with thanks:

E. P. Dutton & Co., Inc.:

Lines from the book CONCH OF BEES by Luke Zilles, copyright 1956 by
E. P. Dutton & Co., Inc. Reprinted by permission of the publishers.

Faber and Faber, Ltd.; and Harcourt, Brace and Company, Inc.:

Lines from the plays *The Family Reunion, Murder in the Cathedral* and *The
Rock*; and lines from the poems "The Dry Salvages" and "East Coker." Reprinted from THE COMPLETE POEMS AND PLAYS by T. S. Eliot, with the
permission of the publishers.

Henry Holt and Company, Inc.:

Lines from COMPLETE POEMS OF ROBERT FROST. Copyright, 1930,
1949, by Henry Holt and Company, Inc. Copyright, 1936, 1948, by Robert
Frost. By permission of the publishers.

Little, Brown & Company:

Lines from FURTHER POEMS OF EMILY DICKINSON, copyright 1929 by
Martha Dickinson Bianchi, by permission of Little, Brown & Company.

Princeton University Press:

Lines from ANCIENT NEAR EASTERN TEXTS RELATING TO THE OLD
TESTAMENT, edited by James B. Pritchard.

Charles Scribner's Sons:

Lines from "Ballade of the Listless Court Ladies," copyright 1953 by Rolfe
Humphries. Reprinted from POEMS, COLLECTED AND NEW by
Rolfe Humphries with the permission of Charles Scribner's Sons.

Lines from THE FIRST MORNING: NEW POEMS by Peter Viereck, copyright 1952 by Peter Viereck. Reprinted by permission of Charles Scribner's Sons.

Twayne Publishers:

Lines from THE DOUBLE ROOT by John Holmes, by permission of the
author and publishers.

To one who taught me
there is no lonely sorrow.
S.T.

Contents

Introduction 13

Chapter one The Occasion of the Poem 23

Chapter two The Fear and Fascination
of Death 40

I The Attraction of
Nothingness 41
II The Nothingness of
Friendship 50
III Nothingness and Divine
Love 57

Chapter three The Failure of Monotheism 66

I "All Men Are Sinners" 69
II "Thy Children Have
Sinned" 78
III "Thou Art the Man!" 83
IV "Art Thou the First
Adam?" 87
V "Can a Man Be Profitable
unto God?" 93

Chapter four The Folly of a God-man 101

I There Is No Mediator 102
II There Is No Resurrection 117

Chapter five The Need for a Christ 133

I "My Witness Is in
Heaven" 134

Contents—Continued

II "I Know My Redeemer Liveth" 142

Chapter six   **The Ignorance and Arrogance of Religion** 156

I The Anomaly of Happiness ... 156
II The Absence of God 160
III The Tragedy of Integrity ... 168
IV The Inaccessibility of Wisdom 170
V The Religious Claims of Morality 175

Chapter seven   **Risking the Storms of God** 189

I Introduction in Prose and Verse 190
II Grace Through an Intercessor 193
III The Ways of God 199
IV The Giver of Songs in the Night 203
V The Mercy of the Creator ... 208
VI The Lord of the Seasons ... 211

Chapter eight   **The Irony of Love and Faith** 218

I The First Discourse of the Lord 219
II The Second Discourse of the Lord 230

Selected Bibliography 251

Index of Passages 253

A Word on Quotation from Scripture

The poetry of Job is reproduced in this book substantially in accordance with the King James Version, which has been conservatively amended whenever errors or obscurities warranted a change.

Demonstrations of the proposed renderings have generally been omitted so as not to clutter the enjoyment of the verse with notes of a technical nature.

JOB:

Poet of Existence

Introduction

Hoc lege quod possit dicere vita meum est.
Read this of which life can say, " 'Tis my own."
Martial, *Epigrams,* X, 4, 8.

JOB, more than any other book of the Bible, belongs to the literature of the world. Yet, how many read this poem in our day? Classics bear the burden of greatness. Did not Mark Twain define a classic as "something that everybody wants to have read and nobody wants to read"? It may be that in the realm of books as of men fame impedes familiarity and eminence engenders fear. The frequentation of masterpieces is hazardous, for it may stir one from indolence and move him to action.

We do not mind a book which incites our admiration, provided it leaves our freedom unimpaired. We recoil from any volume which transgresses the bournes of aesthetics and makes us feel uncomfortable about life or ourselves. We are able to endure the proximity of greatness only when we manage at the same time to preserve our sense of security and our illusion of independence. To read a classic is to take a risk, for a classic always possesses a potentiality of disruptiveness.

There may be another reason for the neglect of masterpieces. They were often written by poets, and the poetic idiom is never readily accessible. Twentieth-century man, in particular, tolerates a brush with literary magnitude only when he can grasp it with a minimum of effort. Who will, in our age, consent to toy for more than a moment with a piece of art that resists casual wooing? Yet a true poem, like a true woman, will not yield to any passer-by. As Mr. Randall Jarrell noted:

> . . . It is not just modern poetry, but poetry, that is today obscure. *Paradise Lost* is what it was; but the ordinary reader no longer makes the mistake of trying to read it—instead he glances at it, weighs it in his hand, shudders, and suddenly, his eyes shining, puts it on his list of the ten dullest books. . . .[1]

We treasure masterpieces on the word of our forebears who bequeathed them to us, while we too often dismiss them because they require of us too strenuous an effort of comprehension. "A book is never a masterpiece," wrote the brothers Edmond and Jules de Goncourt in their *Journal,* "it becomes one." Likewise, a book that has long been a masterpiece may fall into oblivion if men of a new age refuse to learn its peculiar diction.

Of such is Job, today unknown even by some who claim no immunity to cultural urges. Incidentally, that this classic happens to belong to the Bible does not explain its quality of *terra incognita,* for it is neglected also by those members of both church and synagogue who daily read other portions of Scripture.[2]

Tennyson heralded it, somewhat extravagantly, as "the greatest poem, whether of ancient or modern liter-

[1] *Poetry and the Age* (New York: Alfred A. Knopf, Inc., 1953), p. 3.
[2] Israel J. Gerber's survey, in *The Psychology of the Suffering Mind* (New York: The Jonathan David Co., 1951), pp. 33-35.

ature." Carlyle, with little more sense of measure, hailed it as "one of the grandest things ever written with pen." It may be that such praise is today worse than condemnation.

I

The poem of Job has usually been approached either as a book of edification or as a tract of skepticism. Some have seen in it merely a discussion of innocent suffering and a plea for patience under duress. Others have thought it was an attempt to

> ... assert eternal Providence,
> And justify the ways of God to men.[3]

Still others have praised it as a monument of revolt against the tyranny of dogma. A generation ago the verdict of most independent exegetes could be summed up in Morris Jastrow's sentence, "The questioner scans the heavens and finds the supposed throne of mercy without an occupant."[4]

Contemporary interpreters are looking for a new understanding of the book as cultural trends make our generation eager for its reappraisal. This classic of Hebrew poetry offers a challenge to the modern mind for it views life without illusion, but not with despair. It punctures traditional beliefs in God, but not in faith. It sees the futility of death, but not of creation. It lifts man from the plight of meaningless existence by inserting him into

[3] John Milton, *Paradise Lost*, I, 25-26.
[4] Morris Jastrow, Jr., *The Book of Job* (Philadelphia: J. B. Lippincott & Co., 1920), p. 28.

the context of the *Opus Dei*. It points to a God beyond
the God of ethical concept. It resolves the irony of doubt
by depicting human life as an active contemplation. It
overcomes tragedy by viewing man in the perspective of
divine creativity. It offers a theology of creative participation.

II

Times are singularly ripe for a rediscovery of Job.
First, we have witnessed the birth and growth of depth
psychology. Freud and his followers, many of whom
were steeped in the Hebraic thought forms, have
brought a revolution in our understanding of human
nature. They have uncovered the recesses of the uncon-
scious and bared the vulpine elements which lurk below
the threshold of consciousness—incidentally, a Hebraic
metaphor (Gen. 4:7). Psychotherapeutic methods alone
may fail to save man from the vacuity or the meaninglessness of life under the sun, but they can prepare him
to look at his own existence *sub specie aeternitatis*. Their
diagnosis, at once trenchant and reassuring, clears a path
toward lucidity about the self and honesty toward others.
It cuts a trail through the Victorian jungle of hypocrisy.
It creates a simple and otherwise inaccessible virtue—
perspicuity and acceptance. So does the poet of Job,
against the moralism and the ecclesiasticism of all ages.

Second, we have been exposed to explorations and ex-
periments in poetry, drama and novel. Poets like Valéry,
Aragon, Emmanuel, Eliot, Auden, Marianne Moore;
dramatists like Pirandello, Sartre, Marcel, Giraudoux,
Montherlant, Anouilh, O'Neill, Tennessee Williams;

novelists like Proust, Gide, Kafka, Mauriac, Faulkner, Steinbeck, Wilder, Camus, have gone and are going far beyond the generations that have preceded ours in analyzing the loneliness of man in the universe, the hostility of man toward man, and the enigma that man is to himself. They have plotted the "waste land" in which we live or merely exist. Countless are those among us who recognize their own utter solitude when they read, for example, the words of Thomas Wolfe,

Naked and alone we came into exile. In her dark womb, we did not know our mother's face; from the prison of her flesh have we come into the unspeakable and incommunicable prison of this earth. Which of us has known his brother? Which of us has looked into his father's heart? . . . Which of us is not forever a stranger and alone?

Peculiar indeed is an epoch when secular poets and writers, starting apparently from an artistic vantage point, offer a picture of the human situation far more somber and yet convincing than did hell-and-brimstone revivalists of an age gone by. The poet of Job can speak to a generation like ours, which has pierced the bubbles of nineteenth-century belief in the infinite capacity of man for goodness and progress through the spread of education and technology.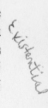

Third, and in parallel fashion, existentialist philosophers join hands with psychologists and littérateurs in revolting against systems of interpretation and knowledge that emerged from the Renaissance or the Enlightenment and received impetus from the thriving of natural sciences. At the turn of the century, Miguel de Unamuno read Pascal and Kierkegaard and he wrote

The Tragic Sense of Life. From Heidegger, Buber and Jaspers to Sartre and Marcel, existentialists attempt to go beyond the conceptual methods of expression and to discern the residue of reality grasped in existence as lived. With courage and sometimes recklessness, contemporary thinkers face the isolation of man in the cosmos, send him "on the road," bring him "to the ridge," give him "thirst," make him "wait for Godot." To be sure, the very nature of philosophical search, which is bound to the "here and now," compels many of them to leave man alone within the finiteness of his anxiety and at the mercy of his own resources, which end with a spadeful of earth. Nevertheless, they have made him aware of his desire for the ultimate. They have revealed to him his quest for being, above the fluctuations of time and beyond the frustration of death. The poet of Job raised the existential questions. He spurned traditional answers and risked theological death in order to confront life in the raw.

Fourth, the whole realm of art presents another facet of our culture which discloses modern man's longing for unity and harmony in the midst of a civilization slipped awry. Needs of the individual for recognition and community appear clearly in many forms of aesthetic endeavor. Painting, sculpture, architecture, music and choreography have in the twentieth century exploded the puffiness and artificiality in which too many aesthetes of the nineteenth century have indulged. Modern artists portray ruthlessly the fragmentary and barren aspects of a mechanistic world; but the new concepts of beauty within the sordid or the plain, unless they reflect a vision that transcends man—as they sometimes do—have only stressed in tone, form, movement and color the dead end of our lives when we live them in an empty universe. Still, contemporary art forms are pointing beyond themselves. They show that the cult of beauty for its own sake exacerbates man's desires without assuaging them. They testify to his wistfulness for the reconciliation and the permanence of the self within an organic community. They proclaim the tragedy of man's alienation from the world he has mastered and they call for his reinsertion within a nature that would be neither his mistress nor his slave. The poet of Job, by lifting his buffeted hero from the curse of birth to the contemplation of a purposeful God at work in cosmic harmony, relates psychology to aesthetics in a manner which strikingly answers the search of contemporary art.

Fifth and last, we have been brought face to face with the so-called theology of crisis, born out of the First World War and spread to American shores by the Depression and the Second World War, if not the threat of a third, with its stone-age eventuality. Karl Barth, Emil Brunner, Paul Tillich, Reinhold Niebuhr and others have placed before the culture of our time the issues of faith with a degree and a quality of urgency which has perhaps not been experienced by the Western world since the time of the Reformation. Best sellers and some fashionable preachers to the contrary, pagan is the kind of religion which caters to the utilitarian demands of our civilization. No one should dare any longer to justify the worship of God on the ground of its psychological helpfulness and still appeal to the Bible. The defense of Jewish or Christian faith and the establishment of its validity on the basis of its pragmatic success should be recognized for what it is: an idolatry. God is not the projection of man's idea of goodness or security. "Doth Job

fear God for nought?" This is the satanic question which
is answered in the negative by those who think they must
support the church because it is the cornerstone of de-
mocracy, a buttress of moral character, a source of peace
for the mind—or is it for the soul?—and a technique for
the pursuit of happiness.

III

The poem of Job stands at the very core of the Bible
and says this hard, shocking word, "It does not pay to be
religious." But then, it also proclaims the biblical truth
par excellence: God is not a mere adjunct of a social
group, be it Israel, the church, the United States of
America or Western culture. However loyal one is to
such historical agencies, and however constructive the
function they may fulfill in the epic of mankind, Israel,
church, country or Western culture is only a relative
means toward an absolute end: the purpose of a creative
God in the universe. Such a truth hurts. Some call it
subversive. In the end, however, it alone can undercut
the attacks which are perennially made against faith in
God. When a Bertrand Russell charges that theistic
belief is merely "a help in church work and in procuring
victory in man-made wars," here comes the poet of Job,
echoed by Second Isaiah, Jesus and Saint Paul, with a
faith in a Deity who transcends all human interests and
even morality.

The ancient Hebrew poem is modern, for it proffers
a plea for pure religion. It says in effect, "God really
hates religion." It shows that there is no sin like religious
sin. As Karl Barth put it, "Religion is the KRISIS of cul-

ture and of barbarism. Apart from God, it is the most dangerous enemy a man has on this side of the grave."[5] Job discovers a new dimension of sin and therefore can understand and receive grace. This has little to do with the so-called "positive thinking" but it generates a positive attitude toward life. It is also more than a mere concern for the ultimate. It is an act of surrender to a divine person, the maker of nature and my creator, and the surrender is a birth.

The poet of Job did not attempt to solve the problem of evil nor did he propose a vindication of God's justice. For him, any attempt of man to justify God would have been an act of arrogance. But he knew and promoted in the immediacy of God's confrontation *a mode of life.* In the very pangs of insecurity, his loss gave him a sense of triumph. He accomplished even more. If it be true that, in the words of Bernhard Duhm, *"er hat seine Dichtung mit seinem Herzblut geschrieben,"* "he wrote his poem with his own blood," then he succeeded in overcoming the subjectivism of his own experience by casting its expression in an artistic form which transcends his culture and makes it valid for our own. Thus, he not only takes his place among all those who suffer, fighting with the incomprehensible forces of evil in the *noce oscura,* but he also can speak to all sufferers an authentic word of comfort, begetting in them the virtue of serenity over woe.

For he knew grief as any man, but he did not enter into a final partnership with what Melville called "the heartless voids and immensities of the universe." On the contrary, he transmuted the taste of sorrow into the

---

[5] *The Epistle to the Romans* (London: Oxford University Press, 1938), p. 268.

knowledge of joy. Not the shallowness of gaiety, to be sure—although his tone, however grim, was never far away from humor—but the depth of a joy brought by the presence of one who moves and warms the worlds.

And we who read Job may likewise find a gain in the loss of self-sufficiency. "As pain that cannot forget," wrote Aeschylus, "falls drop by drop upon the heart, and in our despite, against our will, comes wisdom to us by the awful grace of God."

Chapter I

The Occasion of the Poem

A PECULIAR AURA of veneration tinged with diffidence
surrounds the whole book of Job. This is due, in all
probability, to a misapprehension of the way in which it
was composed, and subsequently to a confusion between
the meaning of the ancient folk tale (1:1—2:13; 42:7-
17) and that of the poem proper (3:1—42:6).

Everyone has heard of "the patience of Job" (James
5:11), but who pays heed to his impatience? Who listens
to his shouts of blasphemy? Who especially ponders on
the irony of God's probing "from the whirlwind" and
queries the reticence of the hero's final assent?

Vaguely acquainted with the story of a man of faith,
we usually ignore the poem of his doubt. Remembering
the plot of the folk tale in prose, we too often neglect the
dialogue in verse. Yet, the poetic discourses are the
raison d'être of the book, and the popular narrative that
surrounds them is only the occasion of the poem.

Here may be witnessed a situation exceptional in the
history of literature. It was in all likelihood the story of

23

Job's patience which enabled the poem of his impatience to survive. From the standpoint of Hebrew-Christian orthodoxy, the poem was highly offensive,[1] and it was preserved only because its prose framework upheld the orthodox doctrine of divine retribution. However disturbing may have been the hero's cries of revolt in the poem, their effect was counteracted—so it was probably hoped—by the example of faith at all cost which was offered by the story. Job may have spoken rashly in the poem, but he repented and the Lord rewarded him in the end. The scheme of divine justice was safeguarded.

In a paradoxical way, it is now the prose story of Job's piety which fails to sustain the interest of modern man and thus drives him to ignore the poem of Job's impiety. Yet it is precisely the poem of Job's impiety which is pertinent to modern man's predicament.

I

Folk Tale of the Man from Uz, 1:1—2:13; 42:7-17

The prologue and epilogue in prose (1:1—2:13; 42:7-17) quite properly arouse in us, together with an appreciation of their dramatic mastery, a feeling of suspicion. A prince is brought low and preserves his serenity. A "good man" is hit and keeps his trust in provi-

[1] This may be inferred not only from the examination of the text itself but also from the accumulation of external evidence. For example: the smooth renderings into Greek made of many Hebrew passages by the Septuagint translators in the second century B.C.; the discussions at the synod of Jamnia (ca. A.D. 95), when the book of Job was finally included in the third canon of the Hebrew Bible; the multitude of marginal corrections proposed in the Hebrew manuscripts by the Masoretes (scribes who wrote down the oral tradition or *masorah*).

dence. On the one hand, one admires the heroism of acquiescence revealed by the hero when he exclaims in his misery,

> Naked came I forth out of my mother's womb,
> And naked shall I return thither:
> The Lord gave, and the Lord hath taken away;
> Blessed be the name of the Lord (1:21).

On the other hand, the spectacle of steadfastness does not arrest the modern temper for long, nor does it lend itself, at any time in history, to artistic elaboration. Contemporary man salutes the sublimity of faith but wonders whether it is accessible to the victim of such horrid fate.

Furthermore, one cannot help being disturbed by the theological implications of the story. What kind of divine being is portrayed here? For the sake of winning a wager over a cynic in the heavenly council, or at best in order to prove the reality of disinterested devotion among men, the Deity allows that his best servant be brought to destitution and torture. Surely—not a few will muse—the mystery of human suffering is too perplexing and too shocking a matter for even a God to use it with such levity. The prologue, whatever its literary sweep and dramatic verve may be, offers an archaic and—to many minds—intolerable theology.

Thus Robert Frost, in *A Masque of Reason,* chides the Creator for having carried out the Joban experiment. The following exchange is imagined between God and Job after the trial is over:

God . . . .
       I was just showing off to the Devil, Job,

As is set forth in chapters One and Two.
(Job takes a few steps pacing.) Do you mind?
(God eyes him anxiously.)

Job   No. No, I mustn't.
'Twas human of You. . . .[2]

The epilogue is even more remote from the realities
of existence than the prologue. For a reward, Job receives again his health, twice over his lost property, fourteen sons instead of seven,[3] and three daughters as before.

And he called the name of the first, Dove; and the name
of the second, Cinnamon; and the name of the third,
Perfume-horn. And in all the land were no women
found so fair as the daughters of Job; and their father
gave them inheritance among their brethren. After this
lived Job a hundred and forty years, and saw his sons,
and his sons' sons, even four generations. So Job died,
old and full of days (42:14-17).

Modern minds will enjoy the consummate art of this
oriental yarn and appreciate the quaintness of the folk-
loric motifs; but will they find this ending relevant to
the human situation as they know it?

II

Literary analysis shows that the book of Job, in its
present form, is the product not of a single author but of
a school of storytellers, poets, sages and editorial scribes,

[2] Robert Frost, *A Masque of Reason* (New York: Henry Holt and Co., 1945), pp. 16-17.
[3] The Hebrew text probably reads a dual form of the number "seven" (cf. Targum), although the spelling of the word may represent a dialectical form of the singular.

who worked for perhaps as long as a dozen generations on a single theme in a fashion typical of the Ancient Near East.[1]

If we are able, for a moment, to forget Western concepts of literary composition, according to which writing is a highly individual affair, we shall imagine the meaning and the implications of what may be called "sociological authorship." Even today, among pure nomads, a Bedouin poet may be the creative agent within his clan, but his poetic activity is stimulated, encouraged, checked, corrected, challenged or endorsed by the community of his listeners, night after night, around the campfire. The stories and the poems of an individual genius represent the highly complex "give-and-take" of weeks or months of nightly exchanges. The tribal poet may be asked by the sheik to compose a poem in the honor of a guest. He will begin by repeating hackneyed lines which everyone knows by heart, usually some antique love song. Fairly soon, he will insert an original couplet, and the crowd will chime in, chanting the new lines after him if these fit the taste of the moment. A sensitive poet will discern at once whether or not his original creation of the evening meets with approval. If it does, he will repeat his new lines the following night, thereby fixing them in the tribal memory. Otherwise, he will drop them from his repertoire and they will be forgotten. Slowly the poem is built up. Is it the work of a single genius? Yes, because there is indeed one man who towers over his group by his poetic inspiration and skill, his gift and his "knack" for turning a phrase which

[1] For a summary of the many hypotheses which have been proposed on the composition of the book, see Samuel Terrien, "Introduction and Exegesis of the Book of Job," *The Interpreter's Bible*, Vol. III (New York and Nashville: Abingdon Press, 1954), pp. 877 ff.

will catch the attention of his audience at the right instant. No, because without this "touch-and-go" dialogue with a highly articulate and artistically sophisticated community, the individual creator would not receive the stimulus which activates his poetic inspiration. Moreover, the concept of sociological authorship implies not only the collaboration of a tribal group at a given moment of history but also the work of oral transmission, addition, purification and copyright-like fixation which is furnished by many generations of folk singers in the course of centuries.

III

If we attempt to reconstruct the growth of a story and of a poem like that of Job, we are of course reduced largely to conjectural speculation. Nevertheless, internal as well as external evidence suggests that the original story—not the poem—was told as early as the second millenium B.C. around the campfires of shepherds and caravan drivers on the edge of the Fertile Crescent in northwestern Arabia. It probably arose among some tribesmen of Edom, south and southeast of the Dead Sea, who lived, like the hero, on the fringe "between the desert and the sown" and led a semipastoral, semiagrarian mode of existence. That a historical event was at the basis of the tale, there is little doubt.

At the beginning of the sixth century B.C., the Judean prophet Ezekiel spoke of Job, together with Noah and Daniel, as men of old, famous for their righteousness (Ezek. 14:14, 20). In the first part of the fourteenth century B.C., a letter sent to an Egyptian Pharaoh by a Canaanite king mentions a certain Ayab (in Akkadian,

this name corresponds to the Hebrew *Iyyob,* "Job"),
prince of Ashtartu in Bashan, who may well have been
the same historical figure as the biblical hero, although
this of course cannot be proved.[1]

Perhaps handed down from generation to generation
in oral form and possibly in the Edomitic dialect, the
story was at last written down in Hebrew some time between the eleventh and the eighth centuries B.C.,[2] when
it became a part of the national heritage of Israel. Its
dramatic flair placed it on a level with the best epic traditions of the Hebrew literature, such as those of Sarah's
laughter behind the tent post, Jacob's fight at the ford
Jabbok, or the saga of Joseph welcoming his brothers in
Egypt. Whimsically, it depicted the Lord bantering at
the heavenly council with "the satan," a shady character
whose function was apparently to spy on human beings
and to suspect the purity of their motives. The Deity
boasted about the disinterestedness of his servant Job;
from then on, the plot unfolded itself with inevitable

[1] See W. F. Albright, "Two Little Understood Amarna Letters from the
Middle Jordan Valley," *Bulletin of the American Schools of Oriental Re-
search,* No. 89, February 1943, pp. 7-15. Bashan is the fertile region of northern Transjordan, south of Damascus, where a Christian tradition, from the
fourth century A.D., locates the biblical story of Job. The land of Uz (1:1)
had already been located in the same vicinity by the first-century (A.D.) Jewish historian, Flavius Josephus, but this identification was probably made
on the strength of a biblical genealogy (Gen. 10:33) in which Uz is presented
as a son of Aram (Syria, Damascus). More probably, the land of Uz should be
situated in Edom, possibly around the site of 'Is, north of Petra, south of the
Dead Sea. The other geographical names of the folk tale—Teman, Shuah,
Naamah (2:11)—belong to the general area of northwestern Arabia which
surrounds Edom proper. Elsewhere in the Old Testament (e.g., Lam. 4:21),
Uz is also related to Edom. Furthermore, the Edomites were famous for their
"wisdom." This means that they were interested in formulating poetically
their reflections on life, and that they composed riddles, maxims, proverbs,
parables and fables, all of the gnomic genre (I Kings 4:30-31; Jer. 49:7; Prov.
30:1 ff.; Baruch 3:22-23; see Robert H. Pfeiffer, "Edomitic Wisdom," *Zeit-
schrift für die alttestamentliche Wissenschaft,* XLIV, 1926, 113-125; Terrien,
ibid., pp. 878-879).

[2] The language and style of the story present affinities with those of the
early source of the book of Samuel (about 1000 B.C.).

velocity. The whole story was told with stylized devices: one messenger followed another who was yet speaking until woes piled up from the four corners of the horizon. The victim did not falter in his misery and he received at the end a double compensation.

The purpose of such a story, however, was not to describe the character of God. It was to raise the issue of selfless piety. (It did not ask the question, "Why does God permit undeserved suffering?" Rather, it reflected on the query, "Is there among men an exquisite love of God which is not a calculating love?" The story showed itself to be at once naïvely optimistic and yet pessimistic, for it answered, "Yes, there is such a love among men, but quite exceptionally so. Once upon a time, there lived a man in the land of Uz. .) ."

Thus, the folk tale should not be hastily condemned for disclosing an archaic mythology or betraying in its denouement a moralistic view of existence—which in effect defeats the purpose of the plot—but it should, on the contrary, be appreciated for what it is / a parable on pure faith.)

A parable is not an allegory, in which every detail possesses some hidden meaning which one can uncover with the use of a decoding key. A parable has mainly one lesson to teach, within the dress of a homely plot which is developed with circumstantial concreteness, and so does the story of the man from Uz, "Doth Job fear God for nought?" (1:9.)

IV

It was during the first half of the sixth century B.C., a time of national catastrophe and dishonor, that a

Judean genius, who remained nameless, borrowed this story as the occasion of his poem.[1]

Nebuchadnezzar, king of Babylon, had just put an end to the kingdom of Judah. Jerusalem had fallen after a long siege (587-586 B.C.). The temple of Solomon had been burned to the ground. The land had been raped by the soldiery of the world. Members of the Davidic family were murdered or driven to the prisons of distant Babylonia. Priests and princes, professionals and skilled workers, even common laborers and peasants had been marched a thousand miles to ghettos like that of Telabib in southern Mesopotamia. Others had managed to escape to Egypt, Lebanon and the Arabian desert.

Abruptly separated from cultus, kingship and land, when these props of national culture had been pulled out from under them, the Judeans did not disintegrate sociologically and religiously within a hostile culture, as the northern Israelites had done a century before them under the onslaught of the Assyrians (722 B.C.). They became the Jews.

While many gave way to despair, some found comfort in quietism, chanting in the elegiac rhythm,

> It is good to hope and silently to wait
> For the deliverance of the Lord (Lam. 3:26).

Others swore their allegiance to their past and composed some of the best poems of the Psalter,[2] singing,

[1] The Joban poet should be placed chronologically between the prophet Jeremiah (626-582 B.C.), whose confessions he knows and adapts (cf. Jer. 20:14-18 with Job 3:3-26 and Jer. 12:1-3 with Job 21:7 ff., etc.), and the anonymous prophet of the exile called Second Isaiah (about 550-540 B.C.) who was heavily influenced by him. For a technical discussion of the composition and date, see Terrien, *op. cit.*, pp. 884 ff.

[2] See Terrien, *The Psalms and their Meaning for Today* (Indianapolis and New York: The Bobbs-Merrill Company, Inc., 1952), pp. 125 ff.

By the rivers of Babel,
There we sat and wept
As we remembered Zion.

.   .   .   .   .   .

If I forget thee, Jerusalem,
Let my right hand wither! (Ps. 137:1, 5.)

Still others looked toward the future and prepared for
the rebirth of the nation as a religious community. Ezekiel made an architect's plan for a new temple (Ezek.
40:1 ff.), and his disciples edited for the renewal of its
cultic service an elaborate ritual (Lev. 12:1 ff.).

The poet of Job was different. He ignored cultus,
temple, law, covenant, Messiah, even the concept of the
chosen people. He approached the enigma of man's
fate in the world in terms of universal humanity.

In order to accomplish his task he borrowed the story
of the man from Uz. It was foreign and ancient, thereby
providing a pure specimen of manhood, detached from
the particularism of religion and culture. As his contemporaries asked, "Should we really serve God for
nothing in return?" he pointed to Job, a hero of exceptional nobility brought down to a destitution and a pain
of exceptional horror.[3]

The poet, however, was not content merely to repeat
a well-known tale. He used it only as a setting for his
original creation. For he actually re-created the hero.
He took him from the stylization of legend and exposed
him to the realism of history. He transformed a model
of suffering into a brother of all sufferers. He saw a
hallowed figure in a fresco, but he painted an outlaw in

[3] Job's ailment was almost certainly not Hansen's disease, commonly called
leprosy. It may have been an unknown tropical disease, producing dermatic
and nervous disorders, which was similar to *pemphigus foliaceus* (see Terrien,
The Interpreter's Bible, Vol. III, p. 920).

the rawness of reality. In the story Job blessed, but in the poem he cursed. In the former Job was a paragon of "submission," a forerunner of *islam,* but in the latter he became a type of man in misery—hit, bewildered, alone and still proud. Only by dragging his character from the loftiness of faith to the depths of doubt was the poet able convincingly to bring forth at the end the dimension of grace and the response of surrender.

V

Cutting the story open at the precise spot where the friends come to comfort the hero (2:13), the poet lent words to the four characters and concluded this lengthy dialogue with the intervention of God speaking "from the whirlwind." Thus the main parts of the poem present themselves as follows:

    I. The sufferer's soliloquy (3:1-26)

    II. The three cycles of the friends' discourses and the hero's replies (4:1—27:23)

    III. The hero's final defiance (29:1—31:40)

    IV. The discourses of the Lord and the hero's surrender (38:1—42:6)

The discourses of Elihu (32:1—37:24) appear to have been the work of a later poet belonging to the Joban school, and so also does the Hymn to Wisdom (28:1-28). If one gives due respect to the oriental practice of "corporate authorship," these poems should be considered now as an integral part of the whole. Indeed, they were most probably inserted as a kind of liturgical "gradual," preparing the hero psychologically for the divine intervention.

Later scribes have introduced numerous corrections

and particularly have reorganized the third cycle of exchanges between Job and his three friends (22:1—27:23). No doubt attempting to reconcile the hero's views with orthodoxy, editors seem to have omitted Job's reply to Zophar's third speech which is now distributed in various fragments and placed in the mouth of Job. A hypothetical reconstitution of the third cycle follows:

Third Speech of Eliphaz	22:1-30
Job's Reply	23:1—24:17, 25
Third Speech of Bildad	25:1-6; 26:5-14
Job's Reply	26:1-4; 27:1-12
Third Speech of Zophar	24:18-24; 27:13-23
Job's Reply	now missing

This conjectural restoration offers a sequence of ideas and of form that are true to the respective characters as known elsewhere in the poetic discussion.[1]

VI

As is well known, the literary form of the philosophic dialogue was made familiar to Western culture through the works of Plato. However, a long tradition of gnomic literature had existed in Asia Anterior and Egypt much before the time of classical Greece. The Joban poet could speak in universal terms and couch his ideas in the form of a dialogue because he belonged to the international movement of wisdom.

Already in the third millenium B.C., men of Mesopotamia and Egypt, later of Phoenicia and Edom, reflected on the meaning of life or death and learned to formulate

[1] For further details on this and other questions pertaining to the text, language, poetic structure and style, see Terrien, *op. cit.*, pp. 888, 892 ff.

their reflections in the poetic form of proverbs, riddles, fables and parables. Some of them invented the structure of the dialogue, in which a man and his friend or a man and his own self—represented as an *alter ego*— argue back and forth about the validity of a certain theme. Unlike the Socratic dialogue, its oriental prototype did not proceed by swift, conversational exchanges, in which a sentence may be curtly interrupted in the true style of "inter-locution." It followed a solemn and fairly regular pace, according to which each speaker, in turn, delivers a short or long oration.

For example, the "Babylonian Acrostic Dialogue on Theodicy"[1] introduces two speakers: a sufferer and his friend. Each man speaks alternately in a strophe of eleven lines. The sufferer begins and ends the conversation and speaks fourteen times. The friend answers thirteen times. The whole poem is therefore made of twenty-seven strophes. The sophisticated character of the piece appears not only in this uniform structure but also in the acrostic sequence of the twenty-seven initial syllables[2] repeated eleven times each, which yield vertically the sentence, "I, Shaggil-kinam-ubbib, the conjurer, bless god and king." And the name *Shaggil-kinam-ubbib* means "O Esagil, pronounce the righteous pure!" Here are the two concluding strophes:

Strophe XXVI

[Friend]   The primeval king, the god Naru, creator of mankind,

[1] See Robert H. Pfeiffer, "A Dialogue About Human Misery," in *Ancient Near Eastern Texts Relating to the Old Testament*, edited by James B. Pritchard (Princeton, New Jersey: Princeton University Press, 1950), pp. 438-440.

[2] The Akkadian script is syllabic rather than alphabetic.

The glorious god Zulummaru, who nipped
off their clay,
The queen who formed them, the divine
lady Mama,
They bestowed upon humanity ingenious
speech:
Falsehood and untruth they conferred upon
them forever.
Enthusiastically they speak of the rich
man's graciousness,
"He is a king! His tutelary deities go at
his side!"
As if he were a thief, they mistreat a
wretched man,
They bestow slander on him, they plot murder against him,
Disloyally they bring every evil upon him
because he lacks *protection;*
Dreadfully they destroy him, they extin-
guish him like a flame.

Strophe XXVII

[Sufferer]   Be merciful, my friend: listen to my woe!
Help me! See (my) misery, and you will
truly understand.
A wise and imploring slave am I.
Help and encouragement I have not ex-
perienced for an instant.
I walked quietly through the squares of my
city,
My voice was never loud, my speech was
low;
I did not raise my head, I looked (down)
at the ground.

> Like a slave I was not glorified in the
> assembly of [*my peers*].
> May the god Ninurta, who . . . , supply
> help!
> May the goddess Ishtar, who . . . , have
> mercy upon me!
> May the shepherd, the sun of the people,
> [*have mercy*].[3]

None of the wisdom dialogues or poems which have
been discovered hitherto in Egypt or in Mesopotamia
may seriously be considered as a source of the Joban
poet. (However, it is significant to observe that all the
known pieces of the dialogue type deal with the same
general theme: the vanity of human life, the fear of
death, the enigma of suffering, and sometimes even the
futility of pious deeds—a bold expression of nonconformism in a social environment dominated by priestly
hierarchy! For example, a whimsical dialogue between
master and slave examines with cold humor the various
occupations of men, such as the pleasures of eating and
drinking, politics, banking, love of women, travel,
house-building, even highly ethical activities such as
the dispensation of wealth to the poor and the forgive-
ness of enemies. Master and slave agree in complete
cynicism that nothing is worth while. This is what they
have to say about religion:

[Master]   "Servant, obey me."
[Servant]—Yes, my lord, yes.
            "Bring me at once water for my
            hands, and give it to me: I will offer
            a sacrifice to my god."

---

[3] Pfeiffer, *op. cit.*, p. 440.

—Offer, my lord, offer.
A man offering a sacrifice to his god
is happy, loan upon loan he makes.
"No, servant, a sacrifice to my god
will I not offer."
—Do not offer (it), my lord, do not
offer (it).
You may teach a god to trot after
you like a dog when he requires of
you, (saying),
"(Celebrate) my ritual" or "do not
inquire (by requesting an oracle)"
or anything else.[4]

It will readily be seen, by these short excerpts, that the
wisemen of Asia Anterior, predecessors of the Greek
tragedians and philosophers, were not easily satisfied
with the official answers of their environment. What is
remarkable is that the literary form of the dialogue appears to have been created precisely by those who discerned the tragic agony or the tragic boredom in human
life.

Quite clearly, the poet of Job was the heir to a long
tradition of gnomic meditation. Not only does he use
the dialogue form, with its ceremonial symmetry, but he
also quotes dozens of proverbs,[5] he knows the world at
large, particularly Egypt,[6] and his vocabulary reflects

[4] Pfeiffer, "A Pessimistic Dialogue Between Master and Servant," in
Pritchard, *op. cit.*, p. 438, St. viii.

[5] Robert Gordis, "Quotations as a Literary Usage in Biblical, Oriental and
Rabbinic Literature," *Hebrew Union College Annual*, XXII (1949), pp. 209-
10.

[6] See especially Paul Humbert, *Recherches sur les sources égyptiennes de
la littérature sapientiale d'Israël* (Neuchâtel: Secrétariat de l'Université, 1929),
pp. 75-106.

the catholicity of his culture as it includes many words of foreign origin.[7]

While the Joban poet was endowed with a cosmopolitan outlook, and this may explain why he ignored Hebraic cultus and covenant, he was beyond doubt Hebraic to the core, for he dealt with the topic which is central to the whole Bible.

VII

In spite of what commentators have said too often, one must affirm that the poem of Job does not attempt to answer the question, "Why do the righteous suffer?" To be sure, the poet offers a subtle and profound analysis of suffering, with the physiological, psychological, social and spiritual disintegration which it produces or from which it originates. In addition, however, and through the medium of suffering, he shows how the self is discovered in relation to society, nature and the ultimate. At the same time, he makes a sharp critique of the traditional formulations of the nature of God, and this leads him to go beyond what is commonly known as "monotheism." Hence, he attempts to define in poetic terms the reality by which men can live in an indifferent, hostile or, at most, meaningless world.

[7] Terrien, *op. cit.*, p. 892.

Chapter 2

The Fear and Fascination of Death

HOW DOES MAN answer the riddle of self and existence? Not in being a marvel of obedience and submission, as Job was in the prose tale when he said, "What? shall we receive good at the hand of God, and shall we not receive evil?" (2:10), but on the contrary in refusing to bless the name of the Deity, in revolting against the faith of his childhood and of his community, in separating himself even from his dearest and most intimate friends, in losing willfully even more than he had lost unwillingly, in repudiating his reputation of honor among his fellow men.

If in the poem Job had spoken glowingly of accepting the will of God, he would have received approval from his community. Indeed, this is exactly the line of conduct which his three friends recommend that he should take. In the prologue, Job had lost his posterity—that is to say, his only hope in immortality—his wealth and his health, but not his reputation as an extraordinary man, a man of faith. He could have safeguarded this reputation. He could have enhanced it. He could have made it even more legendary than it was. But no. Job fell into despair.

This is the supreme irony of the human situation. Faith that does not know despair prevents man from ever forcing the riddle of self and existence; but despair kills faith and, when carried to the extreme, may bring about self-annihilation. Job falls into despair as soon as he rejects simple trust in a loving God. The faith he has expressed in the prologue becomes in the dialogue an unfaith. It becomes an unfaith because Job, in the dialogue, insists not on the love of God but on his own rights and achievements. Without knowing it, he answers in the negative the satan's question of the prologue, "Doth Job fear God for nought?" Throughout the poetic discussion, he repeats again and again, "My right is still with me. I am perfect but God declares me crooked. I am clean and even if my clothes were white as snow, God would throw me down in a ditch and splash them with mud. I shall never abandon the certitude of my integrity. He may kill me but I shall wait for him. I shall maintain my right before him until the end."

Death is therefore the ultimate risk one takes in order to prove one's worth; and Job is tossed about, throughout the dialogue, between the fear of death and its fascination. Before he reaches this dilemma, however, he begins elementally with the fear of life and the attraction of nothingness.

I

The Attraction of Nothingness

Job's Soliloquy, 3:1-26

Job's religion has failed, but not altogether. In the prologue his wife, moved by compassion more than contempt, taunted him, saying, "Curse God and die!" She was proposing in effect a theological method of euthanasia. In the poem, however, if Job no longer blesses God, he does not curse him either. He merely asks to be put out of his misery, yet he never takes any practical measure toward suicide. He calls for death and even "non-being" but he does not curse God. He only curses life, envies the dead and makes his first philosophical quest.

i

3. Let the day perish wherein I was born,
    and the night in which it was said, There is a
    man child conceived.
4. Let that day be darkness;
    let not God regard it from above,
    neither let the light shine upon it.
5. Let them claim it for their own, darkness and
    shadowy gloom;
    let a cloud settle upon it;
    let an eclipse grasp it as a prey.
6. That night—let obscurity possess it;
    let it not be joined unto the days of the year;
    let it not come into the number of the months.
7. That night—let it be barren from loneliness,
    let no shriek of delight be heard therein.

8. Let them curse it that curse the day,
    who are ready to raise up Leviathan.
9. Let them fade, the stars of the twilight thereof;
    let it wait for light but have none,
    neither let it see the eyelids of dawn open.
10. For it shut not up the doors of my mother's womb,
    nor hid sorrow from mine eyes.

ii

11. Why died I not in my mother's womb?
    why did I not expire as soon as I was born?

12. Why hath there been two knees to receive me,
    and two breasts to suckle me?
13. For now should I lie down in stillness,
    I should be asleep and at rest.
14. With kings and counsellors of the earth
    who built desolate places for themselves;
15. Or with princes that had gold
    and silver heaped in their tombs;
16. Or as a hidden untimely birth I had not been;
    as infants which never saw the light.

17. There the wicked cease from troubling;
    and the weary be at rest.
18. There the prisoners are left at ease;
    they hear not the voice of the jailer.
19. The small and great are there alike;
    and the slave is free from his master.

iii

20. Wherefore is light given to him that is in misery,
    and life unto the bitter in soul;
21. Which long for death but it cometh not;
    and dig for it more than for hid treasures;
22. Which rejoice exceedingly,
    and are glad, when they can find the grave?
23. Why is light given to a man whose way is hid,
    whom God hath hedged in as a beast?

24. For my sighing cometh before my bread,
    and my roarings are poured out like waters.
25. For the thing which I greatly feared is come upon
    me,
    and that which I was afraid of hath befallen me.
26. I have neither peace nor tranquillity;
    instead of rest cometh my torment.

This poem should be viewed in its present context: it is more than a cry from the depths; it is a disruption of

seven days and seven nights of silence (2:13). The three
friends have come from afar to comfort the sufferer, and
their silence should not be interpreted as a mark of hostility or even condemnation. The poet quite clearly en-
dorses the validity of the note in the prose tale, "And
none spake a word unto him: for they saw that his grief
was very great" (2:13).

In the opening lament, moreover, Job does not address
his friends at all, nor even by the slightest implication
does he acknowledge their presence. Indeed, the initial
poem deserves to be called a soliloquy, for its very mood
bespeaks the hero's most grievous suffering: his solitude.

The theme of man's isolation in the universe appears
many times in the poem: it is already subjacent to the
opening chords. For the first result of true pain, whether
it be physical or mental, moral and spiritual, is the
breakdown of communication with other men, even with
intimates. The oriental bonds of community have already been symbolically and therefore actually broken
in the note of the tale: "And he sat down among the
ashes" (2:8), just outside the village or the encampment.
The silent proximity of friends did not succeed in renewing the ancient ties. "They recognized him not" (2:12).
Suffering and disease had wrought their changes. Thus
the poem opens with the curse of life.

In the first strophe (3:3-10), Job wishes that he had
never been born. Nights and days are mythopoetically
endowed with personal existence (as in Ps. 19:3). If
only the day of Job's birth—nay, the night of his conception—had never come to pass, if it had not been called
into being by those heavenly creatures which are, according to ancient mythology, the masters of the calendar, if
Leviathan had been stirred up (vs. 8), then chaos would

have overcome the created order and Job would not have received life. The pain he now endures would never have excruciated him.

Here the poet hints at the spiritual disintegration which is beginning to pervert Job's personality. Under the impact of suffering, the hero begins to lose a sense of perspective on life. He almost suggests that the world, as far as he is concerned, might just as well have been nonexistent since it produced only sorrow for him—a thought that has been echoed often in other literatures, as for instance by Shakespeare in *King John:*

> A wicked day and not a holy day!
> What hath this day deserv'd? what hath it done,
> That it in golden letters should be set
> Among the high tides in the calendar?
> Nay, rather turn this day out of the week,
> This day of shame, oppression, perjury:
> Or, if it must stand still, let wives with child
> Pray that their burdens may not fall this day,
> Lest that their hopes prodigiously be cross'd.

It would be too easy to condemn Job's lack of concern for the fate of others, and to regret that pain, leading to isolation, in turn may induce irresponsibility. The poet was aware of the dangers of egocentricity, which is the natural fruit of grief, for he has taken up the theme again in the course of the work.

Some might find it tempting, at least among non-Latin Westerners, to censure Job's outburst as a display of Mediterranean self-pity. Modern psychology, however, has called attention to the therapeutic significance of literary expostulation. There is a seed of healing in the

articulate exteriorization of grief. Alone "the damned
don't cry," said Eugene O'Neill in *Mourning Becomes
Electra.*

The second strophe (3:11-19) introduces a new motif
as it passes from the hatred of life to the love of death.
The ancient Hebrews did not believe in natural immortality. Perhaps in revulsion against the Egyptian
funerary rituals which were destined to insure an after-
death resurrection and which consumed, ironically
enough, most of the energies of the living, Israel accepted for more than a thousand years the early Semitic
idea of near annihilation. Life after the grave was not
believed to be life, indeed, but a gray sort of partial survival, without joy and without peace. Thus, the Old
Testament generally calls for a long life upon this earth
and the Psalmists in particular pray with passion that
death be postponed, since "the dead cannot praise the
Lord." Only with the latest books of the Hebrew Bible
did the idea of a full existence with God after death
gain access to the religious mind of Judaism (Isa. 25-26;
Dan. 12). Conceived through the symbol of the resurrection of the flesh—as the seat of personal identity, emotion, thought and power—this idea of immortality was
radically different from either the early Semitic belief in
partial survival in the grave or the Hellenic concept
of a natural permanence of the human soul. It represented a rebirth through an act of divine re-creation.
This late Old Testament motif found its way into the
faith of the early Christian Church.

At the outset of the second strophe, Job reveals a view
of the afterlife which stands in sharp contrast with that
of the Old Testament in general and is equally distant
from the later Judeo-Christian faith in resurrection.

The sequence of thought is similar to that of Sophocles, who could say a century later in *Oedipus at Colonus,*

> Not to be born is the most
> To be desired; but having seen the light,
> The next best is to go whence one came
> As soon as may be.

For Job at the threshold of the argument, to die is to find an exit from present hell. More, for a prisoner or a slave, it is to receive freedom and even to enjoy the company of the great men of the past. Death is the only genetrix of man's hollow desires for liberty, fraternity, equality. Emily Dickinson, who said,

> Unto the dead
> There is no geography,

might have added, "but a knowledge of history," sublimated in cold promiscuity with the kings and counselors of the earth.

Here is a view of attractive death which is not unlike that of some Egyptian wisemen. The author of the "Dialogue Between the Man Weary of Life and His Soul," for example, was almost tireless in describing the attractiveness of the afterlife:

> Death is in my sight today
> (Like) the recovery of a sick man,
> Like going out into the open after a
> *confinement.*
> Death is in my sight today
> Like the odor of myrrh,
> Like sitting under an awning on a
> breezy day.

> Death is in my sight today
>   Like the odor of lotus blossoms,
>   Like sitting on the bank of drunkenness.
> Death is in my sight today
>   Like the *passing away* of rain,
>   Like the return of men to their houses
>   from an expedition.
> Death is in my sight today
>   Like the clearing of the sky,
>   Like a man *fowling thereby* for what he
>   knew not.
> Death is in my sight today
>   Like the longing of a man to see his
>   house (again),
>   After he has spent many years held
>   in captivity.
>
>
> Why surely, he who is yonder
>   Will be a living god. . . .[1]

Let it be made clear that Job did not accept the Egyptian idea of a resurrection. He toyed with such a hope several times in the course of the poem, but he rejected it even in the famous passage on the living Redeemer (19:25-26). Nevertheless, the second strophe reveals the vigor of his nonconformism. Such a romantic interpretation of death represents man's need for an ultimate security. After Job, many were those who cried,

Would that the womb could have been the tomb of me.

At the moment of extremity in the struggle, here and

[1] John A. Wilson, "A Dispute over Suicide," in *Ancient Near Eastern Texts Relating to the Old Testament, op. cit.,* p. 407.

now, the romantic hero can always command, as did Cleopatra,

> Give me my robe; put on my crown; I have
> Immortal longings in me. . . .

But this represents final self-deceit. In Job, the will "to end it all" does not spring from the attraction of nothingness. "Death is not the opening of a gate," wrote Geoffrey Moore on Swift, "but the closing of a wound." And thus, although Job would not say, with a modern poet like Donald Hall,

> Life is hell, but death is worse,

he is only "half in love with easeful death." He is fascinated, yes, but not enough to follow the advice of his distraught spouse in the prologue. The Joban hero, even in the poem, maintains the will to live. And he can do so because he still stands in a personal rapport with a personal Deity. To be sure, this God is at best a *deus absconditus,* a hidden God, and at worst a hostile God. But Job never brings himself to dismiss the reality of a living God from his world. He feels desperately his isolation precisely because he can ignore neither man nor God.

In the third strophe, therefore, God at last is named (3:20-26). The question "why?" is more theological than philosophical. It is not spoken by a man out of mere intellectual curiosity. It is thrown at the void that surrounds him by a man who has known intimate communion with a God he loved and who now discerns in the character of that same God a dimension of hate. Indeed,

it is not the philosophical problem of evil which moves
the poet. It is rather the deeply religious anxiety that
rises from a doubt over God's intentions for man. At the
same time, Job's return to the awareness of God is simul-
taneous with his fascination for death, but little by little
the awareness of God, even of a hostile God, chases away
the thought of extinction. But the attraction for nothingness is not a superfluous element in the pilgrimage of
suffering. Indeed, this fascination itself may well have
lost its power through its very exercise. "Only those
who have grasped their non-being," says Julius Caesar
in Thornton Wilder's *Ides of March,* "are capable of
praising the sunlight."

Furthermore, Job's quest appears at a moment when
the egocentricity he expressed in the first strophe is no
longer running the risk of deteriorating into social irresponsibility. Just as he becomes again aware of God, so
also he rediscovers, however indistinctly, his solidarity
with the mass of sufferers; and it is in their name that
he speaks as a champion for their cause. His self-centeredness finds a channel into a concern for the lot of
aching humanity.

II

The Nothingness of Friendship
Job's First Reply to Eliphaz, Part I, 6:1-30

The order in which the poem should be read presents
a small problem of real complexity. On the one hand,
one may of course follow the text as it presents itself and
pass from Job's initial soliloquy (ch. 3) to the first speech

of Eliphaz (chs. 4-5), then continue with Job's imme-
diate "reply" (chs. 6-7), etc. Such a method, however,
fails to show the way in which the hero's thought develops, above and within the apparently overlapping
themes.

On the other hand, one may take up together all the
discourses of Job and attempt to discern the unifying
patterns of his ideas. Such a method, however, fails to
show that, although the hero never answers directly or
immediately the arguments enunciated by the friends,
his own interpretation grows not only through the power
of his own inner searching but also in reaction to and
by the stimulus of the friends' suggestions, innuendoes
or attacks.

A compromise between the two lines of approach may
be less disadvantageous than either the former or the
latter. Let us presently postpone the reading of the first
discourse of Eliphaz (chs. 4-5) and continue the study
of the initial soliloquy (ch. 3) by taking up the hero's
reply to the first friend (chs. 6-7). In point of fact, the
poet seems to have devised a technique of delayed reaction in the way Job answers his friends. For example,
while the outburst of chapters 6 and 7 is clearly provoked
by the attitude of Eliphaz in chapters 4 and 5, a specific
retort to the specific arguments of Eliphaz will have to
wait until the hero "answers" Bildad in chapters 9
and 10.

At any rate, the link between chapter 3 and chapters 6
and 7 is evident. Pursuing the same trend of thought,
Job now finds a justification for his desire to die when
his friends fail to bring him a realistic appraisal of the
situation as he knows it and especially the warmth of
human love which could have lifted him up from his

isolation. In a sense, the attraction of nothingness over-
laps with a theme which may be called "the nothingness
of human love," since the poet echoes the "I would not
have been" of the soliloquy (3:16) with the devastating
condemnation of the friends in the phrase, "Thus now
are ye for me nothingness" (6:21).

i

6:2.   Oh that my grief were thoroughly weighed,
              and my calamity laid in the balances together!
    3.   For now it would be heavier than the sand of the
              sea :
              therefore my words have been wild.
    4.   For the arrows of the Almighty are within me,
              the poison whereof my spirit drinketh up:
              the terrors of God do set themselves in array
              against me.

    5.   Doth the wild ass bray when he hath grass?
              or loweth the ox over his fodder?
    6.   Can that which is unsavory be eaten without salt?
              or is there any taste in the white of an egg?[1]
    7.   The things that my soul refused to touch
              are as the bread of my sorrow.[1]

ii

    8.   Oh that I might have my request;
              and that God would grant me the thing I long
              for!
    9.   Even that it would please God to crush me;
              that he would let loose his hand, and tear me off!
   10.   Then should I yet have comfort;
              yea, I would exult with joy in pain unsparing;

[1] Hebrew obscure.

> for I would not have denied the words of the
> Holy One.

11. What is my strength, that I should hope?
    and what is mine end, that I should prolong
    my life?
12. Is my strength the strength of stones?
    or is my flesh of brass?
13. Is it not that my inner resource is nought?
    and that sound wisdom is driven quite from me?

iii

14. Mercy from his friend is due to him that is in
    despair,
    even when he forsaketh the fear of the Al-
    mighty.[2]
15. My brethren have dealt deceitfully as a brook,
    as a ravine of streams that have dried;
16. They were once full from winter's ice,
    and fed with the melting snow;
17. With summer's heat, they vanish:
    when it is hot, they are consumed out of their
    place.
18. Caravans are turned aside from their way;
    they go up to the void, and perish.
19. The caravans of Tema looked,
    the travelers of Sheba waited for them.
20. They were confounded because they had hoped;
    they came thither, and were ashamed.
21. Thus now are ye for me nought;
    ye see my casting down, and are afraid.

iv

22. Did I say, Bring unto me?
    or, Give a present for me of your substance?

[2] Hebrew uncertain.

23. Or, Deliver me from the enemy's hand?
    or, Redeem me from the hand of tyrants?
24. Teach me, and I will hold my tongue:
    and cause me to understand wherein I have
    erred.
25. How forcible are right words!
    but what doth your arguing reprove?
26. Do ye imagine to reprove words,
    and the speeches of one that is desperate, which
    are as wind?

27. Yea, ye would play dice over the fatherless,
    and ye would gamble over your friend.
28. Now therefore be content, look upon me;
    to your faces would I lie?
29. Return, I pray you, let there be no injustice done;
    again I say, Return, my cause is at stake.
30. Is there iniquity in my tongue?
    cannot my taste discern perverse things?

In the first strophe (6:2-7), Job agrees that the
thought of his initial soliloquy (ch. 3) has been rashly
expressed (vs. 3), and he implicitly begs his friends to
exercise understanding and patience. They might discern that the wildness of his language is to be weighed
against the burden of his pain. A tragic hero, by the very
enormity of his fate, may be allowed an impetuosity of
speech which reasonably contented men would never
dream of uttering. A man about to die has earned a privilege of temerity which should be denied a bourgeois
seated in comfort. Suffering is a spur to thinking boldly.
Conventional disguise is a luxury in the last hour. Death
is the moment of truth. Melville wrote: "Tormented
into desperation, Lear, the frantic king, tears off the
mask, and speaks the same madness of vital truth."

For Job, the pain and the grief are further compounded by the solitariness that comes from the failure of the friends, and capped by the ultimate discovery of the hostility of God. In a single sentence, the hero expresses this discovery and sees at once its consequence: his outlook is being distorted into madness.

> The arrows of the Almighty are within me,
>   the poison whereof my spirit drinketh up (vs. 4).

The rhetorical questions that follow reveal the lucidity he still enjoys. He knows, against Eliphaz, that no "conversion" would insure his healing.

Indeed, this hidden thought brings back in the second strophe (6:8-13) the theme of his initial lament. Death remains for him the only cure. Death indeed would be "joy in pain unsparing" (vs. 10), for it would enable him to die in time, before he could repudiate his faith and utter the curse which haunts him.

> So espoused to death, with blood [he would seal]
> A testament of noble-ending love
>   *(Henry V,* iv, 6, 26).

The theme of the fascination of death is now altered. It represents no longer the wish to escape, as in the soliloquy, but, on the contrary, the desire to remain faithful to a God of love—a thought which might give to Shelley's line a new sense:

> Die, if thou wouldst be with that which thou dost seek.

In Job's case, that would be still the possession of his only treasure, the awareness of his integrity. He is going after death, now, not because he hates life, but because he fears, through the disintegration of his personality, the weakening of his will to trust.) Already his inner resources, the equilibrium of character learned as an heir to a noble tradition, the soundness of analytical and introspective faculties, and the ability to decide and to act accordingly (vs. 13) have been driven quite from him.

Is there no help for Job, then, in the presence of his friends? There might have been, if instead of words they had offered genuine affection. The third strophe (6:14-21) opens with one of the most modern statements of ancient literature, whether we read the ambiguous Hebrew of the text as meaning (vs. 14),

Mercy from his friend is due to him that is in despair,
     even when he forsaketh the fear of the Almighty,

or, with several recent translators,

He who withholds kindness from a friend
     forsakes the fear of the Almighty.

The second translation is the bolder and, on textual grounds, less likely than the first.[3] Its thought, however, is attractive to the contemporary mind, which likes to see religious correctness not as an intellectual assent to a creed but as the all-demanding outreach of genuine love. The first translation provides an idea which is almost as intrepid. Job is now warning his friends that affection, when authentic, should not regard the theological position of the person it embraces. Indeed, true love will not stop at heresy but will cherish even the heretic.

Frustration from love expected but denied usually leads to bitterness. Job now compares Eliphaz, Bildad

---

[3] It implies a correction of the Hebrew text on the bases of the Syriac, Vulgate and possibly Targum.

and Zophar to desert wadys, swollen by spring thaw, which soon vanish in the sands with the heat of early summer. They show the way to a void (vs. 18), he says, using one of the words elsewhere applied to primeval chaos; and this may be the reason for which, he concludes, "You are likewise for me become a nothingness" (vs. 21a). The last line of the strophe discloses, as does the first (vs. 14), a shrewdness of psychological observation which might well be placed on the desk of modern counselors:

Ye see my calamity, and are afraid (vs. 21b).

The spectacle of a sorrow that is past human ken and skill creates elemental awe. In addition, the poet may suggest that orthodoxy is often cowardly: would not the gift of sympathy, extended to such a deranged individual, court the wrath of the divine?

The fourth strophe (6:21-30) brings dramatic movement to the scene. The vigor of Job's attack apparently induces the friends to take their leave, and this gesture prompts the twice-iterated request of "Return" (vs. 29). The lamenter is changing into a fighter. He is determined to win his cause.

III

Nothingness and Divine Love
Job's First Reply to Eliphaz, Part II, 7:1-21

The initial theme of death as annihilation is not forgotten. This time, however, the hero neither wishes to

die as a solace nor begs to die as a safeguard. He muses
on the brevity of existence upon the earth, and the fear
of death replaces its fascination. Is not the sense of mortality the prerequisite of hope?

In a display of notable dexterity in thought and of art
in lyrical expression, the poet now moves the hero to
meditate upon God and at last to address that God directly in a style of address usually known as "prayer."
But what a prayer it is! With a humor near to sarcasm
and not without tenderness, Job imagines a God, finally
repentant, who looks for his servant—too late. Divine
love is confronting nothingness.

i

7:1.   Is not man's lot a war service upon earth?
              are not his days also like the days of a hireling?
  2.   As a slave earnestly desireth the shadow,
              and as a hireling looketh for the reward of his
                work;
  3.   So am I made to possess months of emptiness,
              and nights of torture are appointed to me.
  4.   When I lie down, I say, When shall I arise and the
              night be gone?
              and I am full of tossings to and fro unto the
                dawning of the day.
  5.   My flesh is clothed with worms and clods of dust;
              my skin is broken and become loathsome.
  6.   My days have been swifter than a weaver's shuttle,
              and are now spent, without hope.

ii

  7.   O remember that my life is wind:
              mine eye shall no more see good.
  8.   The eye of him that hath seen me shall see me no
              more:

          thine eyes are upon me, and already I am not.

9.   As the cloud is consumed and vanisheth away;
      so he that goeth down to the grave shall come up
         no more.

10. He shall return no more to his house,
      neither shall his place know him any more.

11. Therefore I will not refrain my mouth;
      I will speak in the anguish of my spirit;
      I will complain in the bitterness of my soul.

iii

12. Am I a sea or a sea-monster,
      that thou settest a watch over me?

13. When I say, My bed shall comfort me,
      my couch shall ease my complaint;

14. Then thou scarest me with dreams,
      and terrifiest me through visions:

15. So that my soul chooseth strangling,
      and death rather than my life.

16. I loathe it; I would not live alway:
      let me alone; for my days are a breath.

iv

17. What is man, that thou shouldest magnify him?
      and that thou shouldest set thine heart upon
         him?

18. And that thou shouldest visit him every morning,
      and try him every moment?

19. How wilt thou not depart from me,
      nor let me alone till I swallow down my spittle?

20. If I sin, what do I do to thee, O thou watcher of
      men?
      why hast thou set me as thy mark?
      why have I become a burden to thee?[1]

21. And why dost thou not pardon my transgression,
      and take away mine iniquity?

[1] The MSS. now read "to myself" (this is one of the eighteen corrections of the scribes, who thought such a reading offensive to the Deity).

For now shall I sleep in the dust;
>   and thou shalt seek me in the dark, but I shall
>   not be.

If life were immortal and eternity a joy, the sufferings of these days could be endured, for they would only form a prelude to permanence in delight. But death means extinction. Job muses on two levels at once (first strophe, 7:1-6). On the one hand, he still desires the shadow which will terminate his labors (vs. 1-2) and finds consequently his nights of torture interminable (vs. 3-5). On the other hand, nevertheless, he complains that his days are spent "swifter than a weaver's shuttle," because they are without hope, either of a deliverance here below or of a reversal in the hereafter.

Here is the contradiction which man is dragged to confront in the situation of unfaith. Life is not worth living, for it is not the vestibule of heaven. Yet even if it is hell, give me life! Raskolnikov in Dostoevsky's *Crime and Punishment* exclaims:

Life is only given to me once and I shall never have it again; I don't want to wait for the "happiness of all." I want to live myself, or else better not live at all. . . . Where is it I've read that some one condemned to death says or thinks, an hour before his death, that if he had to live on some high rock, on such a narrow ledge that he'd only have room to stand, and the ocean, everlasting darkness, everlasting solitude, everlasting tempest around him, if he had to remain standing on a square yard of space all his life, a thousand years, eternity, it were better to live so than to die at once! Only to live, to live and live! Life, whatever it may be! . . . How true it is! Good God, how true! Man is a vile creature. . . . And vile is he who calls him vile for that.

The fascination of death has now been swallowed up by its fear. Rather, the fear of misery in this life is overcome by the fear of nothingness. Gone is what T. S. Eliot calls "the lust of self-demolition," for life is too dear. Even the endurance of ostracism from God and men, and the instant by instant negotiation with a "broken skin" and a flesh "clothed with worms," are to be preferred to self-cessation. Perhaps no theme has haunted the imagination of men more often than this. "When I consider," wrote Pascal, "the brief span of my life, swallowed up in eternity past and to come, the little space that I occupy, lost in the immensity of space of which I know nothing and which knows nothing of me, I am terrified and I am astonished that I am here rather than there." Job who calls for strangulation in one moment complains of the brevity of life in another. The fact is that he is slowly being reconciled with existence. He no longer refuses to live, precisely when he discovers, in the words of Kenneth Alling,

life's profound disorder,
Ephemerality.

He does not yet love life, but he now dreads death. Life is an ambiguous value, desirable even when destitute and yet spoiled by its mortality. Byron lends these words to Cain, in the familiar dialogue:

Adam. Dost thou not live?
Cain. Must I not die?

. . . .

I sought not to be born; nor love the state
To which that birth has brought me.

. . . . I live,
But live to die.

Facing the prospect of tomorrow's last breath, the hero turns his impersonal meditation on the fate of mankind into a personal appeal to the God of his erstwhile faith. From all appearances, he now concludes that this God is absent, deaf and mute. To speak of a *deus absconditus* is close to denying his omnipotence and his providence. Yet, the Bible in general and the poem of Job in particular were written by men who are much oppressed by the hiddenness of God, and often their perception of his love arises with the enduring of his torment. Faith has survived the flooding of unfaith. Job cannot forget a God in whose presence he has lived and whose bounty he has enjoyed like that of a father. He therefore indirectly points to God's goodness and concern when he appeals to God's memory.

O remember that my life is wind! (Vs. 7*a*.)

Defiance against friends subsides as the fear of mortality (vss. 7*b*-10) brings man back to a sense of creatureliness. Soon, however, the mood of revolt reappears (vs. 11), and the second strophe (vss. 12-16) depicts the brand of egocentricity which feeds on suffering and solitariness. "Oh lonely death on lonely life!" cries Melville through Ahab, the hero who stands against men and the ultimate void. "Oh now, I feel my topmost greatness in my topmost grief." Stanley Geist comments in his book, *Herman Melville: The Tragic Vision and the Heroic Ideal:* "By his solitary descent into the depths of life, man became a demi-god. But the earth was a place of men, and the act of becoming a demi-god was therefore the act of isolating oneself from men while yet remaining incapable of complete godhead." As Job asks God,

Am I a sea, or a sea-monster? (Vs. 12*a*.)

he singles himself out of the human race and drinks the

heady wine of self-deification. To become the antagonist
of God is to be like God, but not quite. And if one
remains "incapable of complete godhead," one may perhaps fancy oneself in the ludicrous position of an anti-
God. Because his fate cannot be explained by his deeds,
Job inflates his ego to cosmic proportions until he can
ask—not altogether in jest—the God whose creative
power constantly overcomes the forces of disorder personified by the abyss and her watery helpers,

> Am I a sea or a sea-monster,
> that thou settest a watch over me?

Quite independently of the ancient cosmogonic myths,
whose imagery persists throughout the Joban poem, one
may easily recognize in the claims of human nature the
illusion of infinity which the spectacle of the sea provides. Is not the sin of the ethically impeccable re-
ligionist as absymal as his self-esteem? Baudelaire
shrewdly delineates the connection between the marine
image and the mystery of human nature:

> *Vous êtes tous les deux ténébreux et discrets:*
> *Homme, nul n'a sondé le fond de tes abîmes,*
> *O mer, nul ne connaît les richesses intimes*
> *Tant vous êtes jaloux de garder vos secrets!*

> Both of you are discreet and dark:
> Man, none has ever searched thine abysmal depths,
> Sea, none has ever known thine inward riches
> So jealous are you both of your secrets!

The taunt is short-lived for the pain is too sharp (vss.
13-14), and yet the poet cannot leave irony out.
    In the third strophe (vss. 17-21), Job parodies a psalm

where reverence prompts a devoted man to ask, in awe
and gratitude,

What is man that thou art mindful of him
and the son of man that thou visitest him? (Ps. 8:4.)

Job twists the hallowed words and while the psalmist expresses his wonder at the divine concern for so insigni-
ficant a creature as man, Job derides the Creator of the
world for paying so much attention to him. Nevertheless, the mood has changed abruptly from that of the
first and second strophes. The torment of God denies his
absence.

Suddenly, the thought of a possible explanation for
his misery—subtly suggested by Eliphaz in his first discourse (4:7, 17, etc.)—enters the hero's consciousness.
Is he a sinner? But even if he were, how could a human
transgression produce harm upon the maker of the
world? (Vs. 20a.) Is not the characteristic of the divinity
the ability to forgive? *"Dieu me pardonnera, c'est son
métier,"* said Voltaire. Job, more grimly, declares:
Should the Deity, at target practice, use me for a mark?
(Vs. 20b.)

The theme of God's enmity cannot last. The ambigu-
ity of the sufferer's position reveals itself once more as
the poet does not permit himself to follow one motif at
the expense of the others. God the shooter of arrows is
also the God who gropes for man in the dark.

Bewildered, the hero is not able to reconcile intellec-
tually the two poles of his experience, but he knows that
after he dies, the Deity will regret the deed. The Hebrew
verb used in verse 21d, "thou shalt seek me diligently in
the dark," is coined from the noun for "darkness before
dawn" and is often used of passionate longing of men

for God (Ps. 63:1, for example). Job reverses the normal use of the word as he pictures the Deity, groping in the gloom for him—in vain. "I shall not be," he declares, renewing in a dramatic ending the thought already expressed earlier in passing (vs. 8*b*). The love of God is affirmed and denied at the same time. It is affirmed in a context of supreme irony by a man in struggle against himself.

The theme of nothingness has thus been developed with unsurpassed art. First, in the soliloquy, Job was attracted by the kind of escapism which may be found in death, especially when its horror can be veiled for a moment by Egyptian illusions. Second, the theme reappears in an entirely different context. The intervention of society only reveals to Job the brutality of his isolation. Having confronted nothingness in relation to his own destiny, Job now faces a new kind of void—the lack of love. Third, it is God who faces nothingness. As Job's hope in a God who would not let him go regains a hold upon his consciousness, and is contradicted by his observation, he comes close to affirming the reality of the love of God. But this affirmation is immediately withdrawn by the prospect of Job's own death, which only affirms the reality of the hatred of God. Still, love is not canceled by hatred. Just as Job, in the presence of his friends, faced nothingness, so also God, in the scandal of Job's death, will look at the void. With this daring thought, the poet undoubtedly conveys another. In our kind of world, a true God must be a God who suffers.

Chapter 3

The Failure of Monotheism

THE FAITH of Israel received its impetus from the event of the Exodus. The Old Testament as much as the New is the product of a theology of grace. Hebraism as well as Christianity was founded upon a faith in a God who loves man first, not on account of man's achievements or genius, but through the mystery of choice for the fulfilment of a special mission. Both Judaism and the Christian Church, however, while upholding a lofty creed which has been called "ethical monotheism," have in every generation perverted the theology of grace upon which they are historically based into a moralistic and ecclesiastic exclusivism which is divorced from life itself.

From the start, Hebraism reflected upon the mystery of gratuitous love and the scandal of man's response. Why did the Lord choose Israel? Is it because we were more powerful or more numerous or better than other nations? No, we are a stiff-necked people. Does this mean that we may behave as we please? Not quite. The first covenant is clearly conditional.

> Ye have seen what I did unto the Egyptians,
>   and how I bare you on eagles' wings,
>   and brought you unto myself.
> Now therefore, if ye will obey my voice indeed,
>   and keep my covenant,
>   then you shall be a peculiar people unto me
>   above all peoples:
>   for all the earth is mine.
> And ye shall be unto me a kingdom of priests,
>   and a holy nation (Exod. 19:4-6a).

The greater prophets like Amos and his successors, together with the Deuteronomists, the priests during the Exile and the psalmists, because they believed deeply in the omnipotence of a righteous God, understood the ethical implications of the covenant. They declared this covenant abrogated by Israel's rebellion against the divine law. They discerned the connection which unites justice and law. They saw in the catastrophes which swept away Samaria in 722 B.C. and Jerusalem in 586 B.C. the display of retribution in history. They related all ultimate power to their faith in the creator of the universe, and they interpreted the whole of human life and of history in the light of their principle of justice. Animated by a high sense of public and individual morality, they believed in a God who would uphold their own standards of ethics. The wisemen of Israel and Judah, after the time of Solomon, adopted a similar interpretation of existence. Their proverbs proclaimed tirelessly the reward of virtue and the punishment of wicked deeds and intentions. They praised the judge of

all men, the foe of all forms of evil and the champion
of the needy. But the truth of the principle concealed
within it the seed of error.

The friends of Job represent the loftiest form of ethical monotheism, and the poet recognized the nobility
of their positions. To be sure, his sympathy quite clearly
moves toward the lonely sufferer, and the poem must be
autobiographical to a large extent. Nevertheless, he
made a case for the friends, thus revealing a rare degree
of creative imagination and objectivity. The breadth of
his psychological understanding and the compass of his
perspicacity meet with few parallels in the history of
literature. Only some of the Greek tragedians and Shakespeare excel him by the diversity and the complexity of
their psychological analyses. Yet, under the correctness
of their creed and the benevolence of their intention,
the friends of Job merely revealed the failure of ethical
monotheism to cope with existence.

The poet made the friends attractive, the better to
show the fallacy of their beliefs. He was even careful to
indicate that most if not all of their beliefs corresponded
to a large portion of truth. He never opposed the theology of the friends to that of the hero as if the former
were false and the latter true. In effect, he clearly conveyed his conviction that the theological position of the
friends was closely akin to that of Job, thus rendering
the distinction between them the more important because it was the less apparent. But he was also careful
to show that while the theology of the hero was impreg-
nated with life as it grew toward the point when it could
receive and hear the voice from the whirlwind, the magnificent creed of the friends was more akin to the static
preservation of a doctrine than to the pangs of creativity.

Theism, as an intellectual formulation of a belief di-

vorced from faith, loses contact with life. Ethical monotheism, when it provides a method for spelling out
rationally the mystery of God, is utterly separated from
the reality which it seeks to interpret. It negates God
by the very fact that it claims to comprehend him. It
creates an idol in the image of man's mind. The monotheism of the friends has become the mere projection of
their idea of justice.

It is possible that the three names suggest a delineation
of the three friends' respective personalities. Due caution must be exercised at this point, however, for the poet
most probably inherited these names from the ancient
prose tale. Furthermore, he seems to have attempted at
first to produce an effect of psychological diversification
among them, amounting to portraiture; but later on he
lends to all three men indistinctly similar words and sen-
tences, perhaps in an effort to suggest the petrified character of their intellectual positions.

At any rate, the name Eliphaz probably means "God
crushes," Bildad is short for "Darling of God," and
Zophar may be rendered in three playful ways, "Twit-
tering Bird," "Jumping Goat," or "Sharp Nail."

Eliphaz is the eldest of the three and by far the most
learned, the most considerate and the most sophisti-
catedly articulate.

I

"All Men Are Sinners"

The First Discourse of Eliphaz, 4:1—5:27

The first speaker truly offers a masterful oration. It
will be observed that the seven strophes—a sacred num-

ber in the Ancient Near East—are admirably adapted
to the ideas which they present. The first four strophes
form a whole, with chiastic symmetry: three cola followed by two cola in strophes *i* and *ii* become two cola
followed by three cola in strophes *iii* and *iv*. The intermediary development in seven cola forms strophe *v*,
while the third and concluding part of the discourse
contains two identical strophes, *vi* and *vii*, each made
of three times three cola, followed by a refrain introduced by the didactic "Behold!"

i

4:2.   If one assay to commune with thee, wilt thou
         be grieved?
         but from speaking who can refrain?
  3.   Behold, thou hast instructed many,
         and the weak hands, thou hast strengthened.
  4.   Thy words have upholden him who was
         stumbling,
         and made firm the feeble knees.

  5.   But now, it is come upon thee and thou art
         impatient;
         it toucheth thee, and thou art dismayed.
  6.   Is not thy fear of God thy confidence,
         and the integrity of thy ways, thy hope?

ii

  7.   Remember, I pray thee, whoever perished being
         innocent?
         or where were the upright cut off?
  8.   As I have seen it, they that plow iniquity,
         and sow trouble, reap the same.

9. By the breath of God they perish.
    and by the blast of his anger are they consumed.

10. The roaring of the lion, and the voice of the fierce
    lion,
    and the teeth of the young lions, are broken.
11. The old lion perisheth for lack of prey,
    and the whelps of the lioness are scattered
    abroad.

iii

12. A word was brought to me stealthily,
    and mine ear received a whisper thereof.
13. In thoughts from the visions of the night,
    when deep sleep falleth over men.

14. Dread came upon me, and trembling,
    which made all my bones to shake;
15. A breath of air swept over my face,
    and the hair of my flesh bristled up;
16. Someone was standing still, of undiscernible
    aspect;
    a form was before mine eyes;
    There was silence. Then, I heard a voice:

iv

17. "Can mortal man be righteous before God?
    can a strong man be pure before his Maker?
18. "Behold! in his own servants God putteth no trust,
    and his messengers he chargeth with folly!

19. "How much more them that dwell in houses of
    clay,
    and whose foundation is the dust!
    they are crushed like a moth.
20. "Betwixt morn and even they are beaten small;
    without any regarding it, for ever they perish.

21. "Is not their pre-eminence departed from them?
    they die, and not of wisdom!"

v

5:1. Call now: is there any one who can answer thee?
    to which of the holy ones wouldest thou turn?

2. For surely the wrath of God will slay the fool,
    and his zeal will bring the silly one to death.

3. Yea, I have seen the fool taking root;
    but suddenly his abode became rotten.

4. His sons are far from safety;
    they are crushed at the gate, and none shall
    deliver them.

5. His harvest the hungry will eat up,
    or God will take it away by drought,[1]
    and the thirsty will pant after his milk.[1]

6. For affliction cometh not from the dust,
    neither doth trouble spring out of the ground;

7. It is man who begetteth trouble,
    as surely as the sparks fly upward.

vi

8. As for me, I would seek unto God,
    and unto God would I commit my cause;

9. He doeth great things and unsearchable,
    marvellous things without number:

10. He giveth rain upon the face of the earth,
    and sendeth water upon the face of the fields.

11. He setteth the lowly on high,
    and they that mourn are exalted to safety.

12. He frustrateth the devices of the crafty,
    so that their hands cannot perform their enter-
    prise.

13. He taketh the wise in their own craftiness,
    and the counsel of the froward is carried head-
    long.

14. They meet with darkness in the daytime,
    and grope in the noonday as in the night.

[1] Hebrew obscure.

15.   But he saveth from the sword the guileless,
        and the poor from the hand of the mighty.
16.   Thus hope cometh to the destitute,
        and iniquity stoppeth her mouth.

17.   *Behold!* Happy is the man whom God correcteth!
        therefore, despise not thou the chastening of the
          Almighty!

vii

18.   For he maketh sore, but he bindeth up;
        he woundeth, but his hands heal.
19.   From six troubles he shall deliver thee;
        yea, in seven there shall no evil touch thee.
20.   In famine he shall redeem thee from death,
        and in war from the power of the sword.

21.   Thou shalt be hid from the scourge of the tongue,
        neither shalt thou be afraid of destruction
          when it cometh.
22.   At destruction and dearth thou shalt laugh,
        neither shalt thou be afraid of the beasts of the
          earth.
23.   For thou shalt be in league with the stones of the
          field,
        and the wild beasts shall be at peace with thee.

24.   Thou shalt know that thy tent is in peace,
        and thou shalt inspect thy fold, and miss
          nothing.
25.   Thou shalt know also that thy seed shall be great,
        and thine offspring as the grass of the earth.
26.   Thou shalt come to thy grave in full vigor,
        as a shock of grain cometh up in its season.

27.   *Behold!* This we have searched out; it is true.
        Hear it, and know thou it for thy good!

The strophic structure indicates the quality of the
vessel in which the thought is contained. The thought

itself is true to its form, as the speaker moves advisedly
from point to point. He has practiced the fine art of
rhetoric.

First, Eliphaz is intent upon developing the dogma of
divine justice. This dogma forms for him the cardinal
principle of interpretation in Job's case (strophe *i*) or
in the human situation at large (strophe *ii*). The speaker
will not attempt to conceal his disappointment over the
hero's display of self-pity and impatience, but he
broaches the subject with courteous amicableness (vs.
2). Surely, a model of faith and a leader in pastoral
counseling (vss. 3-4) should not fail at the first provocation (vs. 5). Still, Eliphaz refuses to believe that Job
has been stricken for a criminal action. Is not his past
life of piety the guarantee of his eventual return to health
and wealth? (Vs. 6.) The comforter forgets the loss of
sons and daughters for which there can be no compensation. The egocentricity of this understanding of religion
appears at once. Not expressed but clearly implied is a
second view of suffering which will be developed later
(5:1 ff., etc.): if adversity is not a retribution for a
crime, at least it may correspond to a method of education. For the present, the dogma of retributive justice is
upheld by the speaker's empirical observations of life:
"I have seen it" (vs. 8*a*). The innocent may suffer, but
only for a time, and trouble is always the harvest of
iniquity (vss. 7-9). Wild animals may roar in the forest.
When the hunters finally close in upon their dens, the
issue, however delayed, is certain (vss. 10-11).

In the second part of the discourse (strophes *iii* and
iv), Eliphaz appeals no longer to worldly experience
but to supernatural revelation (vss. 12-16). The poetic
adornment, skillful as it is, does not produce the feeling

of instantaneous conviction. Compared to the stylistic nudity of the prophetic visions of Amos (ch. 7) or Isaiah (ch. 6), for instance, the confession of Eliphaz sounds didactic and artificial. Moreover, while the typically Hebraic stories of visual or auditory experiences with revelatory purposes almost always bring man into a direct rapport with the Deity, Eliphaz claims only the vision of "a ghost." Wisdom theology has at a relatively early age stressed the transcendence of God in such a way as to preclude the naïve and compelling, because it is childlike "theophany" or "theophony" common to the patriarchal, Mosaic and prophetic traditions.

The contents of the pseudo-oracle (vss. 17-21) offer likewise a theology of divine remoteness which represents a unilateral distortion of the Hebraic apprehension of God. While the Old Testament generally says, "The Holy One of Israel is in the midst of you," Eliphaz paints a picture of "wholly otherness" in God which may prefigure some aspects of the Moslem creed. In order to exalt the purity of the Deity, the sage of Araby states that even divine beings are not trustworthy and angels are guilty of error (a Hebrew word never used elsewhere in the Bible). Proceeding by *a fortiori* reasoning, the learned man now depicts the human situation. He affirms that man, much lower than the angels, does not deserve on the part of so exalted a God, more respect than a moth. He implies, consciously or not, that finiteness is contiguous with moral corruption (vs. 19). More still, he explicitly denies that God concerns himself with the life or death of any human being (vs. 20). He sows the seeds of a doctrine of divine impassibility. The utter pessimism of his views concerning man's fate finds its climax in the last line of the strophe (4:21). The pre-

eminence of *homo sapiens* does not keep him from final
extinction. Indeed, wisdom itself is an illusion, and man
dies, but not because of an excessive possession thereof!

The god of Eliphaz calls for the remark of William
James: "The stagnant felicity of the Absolute's own perfection moves me as little as I move it." Theological
dogmatism, both in Judaism and in Christianity, has
been partially responsible for the protests—equally mis-
taken—of modern subjectivism. Thus Emily Dickinson,
with soft acidity, could say:

> It's easy to invent a life,
> God does it every day—
> Creation but a gambol
> Of His authority.
>
> . . . . . .
>
> The Perished Patterns murmur,
> But His perturbless plan
> Proceed—inserting here
> A Sun—
> There—leaving out a Man.

It would seem that the concept of the aloofness of God
would prevent Eliphaz from reasserting the doctrine of
retribution; but with apparent unconcern for the inconsistency, he returns to his favorite theme in strophe *v*
(5:1-7). Still pleased with his exposé of divine transcendence, he cannot help referring to it once more as he
asks Job, "If you need help, can you count on intermediary angels or saints?" (Vs. 1.) While a moment ago his
words suggested that creatureliness means sinfulness
(4:19), he now states unambiguously that man is the
author of his destiny. To fit the famed phrase into the
pattern of divine loftiness, one might say that man is not
the captain but the corporal of his soul.

In patent contradiction with his previous declaration
on divine indifference (5:20), Eliphaz now calls upon
Job to pray.

> As for me, I would seek unto God (vs. 8).

The verb "to seek" is used by the prophets and the psalmists alike for the act of worship in the sanctuary. The
unexpressed hint, no doubt, is that Job might, in prayer,
confess his sins—"nothing extreme, mind you, we are all
in the same situation"—and recognize that suffering, if
not in Job's case a direct punishment for a crime, is nevertheless a welcome symptom of the process of *mûsār*
(vs. 17*b*), namely, the corrective discipline through
which youth achieves growth and maturity.

Strophe *vii* contains the peroration (vss. 18-26). To
his empirical experience and his spiritual gifts of special
knowledge, Eliphaz now adds, as he rounds up the
sources of his authority, through investigation and analysis, the communal enterprise of scholars who by "dig-
ging" (vs. 26*a*) have reached a consensus. Speaking now
in the first person plural, Eliphaz is no longer an individual but the mouthpiece of a class. He has convinced
himself of the truth of his diagnosis. He likewise
vouches for the correctness of the prescription. Could it
be that the church may err?

Such is the performance, brilliant but inhuman. The
creed is only partially upheld and no love is conveyed.
Again and again in the history of religions, formulae
which in one generation were true to life became in another a shell deprived of its meat. The professional jug-
gler in apologetics will repulse precisely when he
triumphs. The very people he seeks to reach may admire

the success of his mind but they will also know the failure
of his heart. Cried Hölderlin in *Empedocles*:

> Away! I cannot bear the sight of him
> Who follows sacred callings like a trade;
> His face is false and cold and dead, *as are*
> *His Gods*!

The situation of Eliphaz is made the worse by the fact
that his honesty is not to be doubted. To him may be
applied the words which Beulah, the cook, in Aldous
Huxley's novel, *The Genius and the Goddess,* applies to
a Nobel prize winner, one of the towering personalities
of his generation:

> "Empty, swept and garnished." Those were the words
> that had been given to her. And though it seemed an
> odd thing to say about a man who had more in his head
> than any six ordinary intellectuals, the phrase turned
> out, on second thought, to be an exact description. . . .
> Empty of God, swept clean of common manhood and
> garnished like a Christmas tree, with glittering notions.
> And seven other devils, worse even than stupidity and
> sentimentality, had moved in and taken possession.

The greater prophets, especially Jeremiah, and their
successor, Jesus, recognized the Eliphaz type in the official church of their times. Eliphaz, like most of us, believes in God.

II

"Thy Children Have Sinned"
The First Discourse of Bildad, 8:1-22

The second friend represents a creed which is closely
akin to that of the first, but his approach is different.

Now that Job has shown by his "reply" to Eliphaz (chs. 6-7) that the official creed of society is irrelevant to his situation, preliminaries of oriental etiquette are no longer to be respected. Bildad may have felt that the polite suggestions of his elder colleague were not expressed with sufficient clarity. He will therefore attack the sufferer at the spot where it will hurt: the heart of a father.

i

8:2. How long wilt thou speak these things?
   and how long shall the words of thy mouth be
      like a strong wind?
3. Doth God pervert a right cause?
   or doth the Almighty distort justice?
4. If thy children have sinned against him,
   he hath cast them away into the power of their
      own transgression.
5. If thou wouldest seek unto God betimes,
   and make thy supplication to the Almighty;
6. If thou wert pure and upright;
   surely now he would awake for thee,
   and return happiness to thine innocent home.
7. Thy prosperity of old would appear small indeed
   when compared to the greatness of thy latter
      days!

ii

8. For inquire, I pray thee, of ages gone by,
   and consider the hard-gotten wisdom of their
      fathers;
9. (For we are but of yesterday, and know nothing,
   because our days upon earth are a shadow:)
10. Shall they not teach thee, and tell thee,
    and utter words out of their knowledge?
11. "Can the rush grow without mire?
    can the flag grow without water?

12.   "Whilst it is yet in its greenness, and not cut down,
       it withereth before any other herb."

iii

13.   So are the paths of all that forget God;
       and the hypocrite's hope shall perish:
14.   Whose hope shall be cut off,
       and whose trust shall be a spider's web.
15.   He shall lean upon his house, but it shall not stand:
       he shall hold it fast, but it shall not endure.
16.   He is green before the sun,
       and his branches shoot forth in his garden.
17.   His roots are intertwined between stones;
       he remains alive in the midst of rocks.
18.   But if one uproots him from his place,
       his own house shall swear to him, "I have never
       seen thee."
19.   Behold, this is the only joy of his way:
       Out of his dust shall others grow.

iv

20.   Behold, God will not cast away an innocent man,
       neither will he help the evil doers:
21.   He will yet fill thy mouth with laughter,
       and thy lips with rejoicing.
22.   They that hate thee shall be clothed with shame;
       and the tent of the wicked shall come to nought.

    While Eliphaz had quietly hoped that Job's previous
life of devotion constituted a ground for confidence
(4:6), Bildad at once charges that the sufferer's misfor-

tune is the crop of guilt. He too upholds the dogma of retributive justice, but while Eliphaz had asked,

> Shall mortal man be just before God? (4:17a),

Bildad inquires,

> Doth God pervert a right cause? (8:3.)

The death of Job's sons is sufficient evidence of their criminality. God merely delivered them into the power of their trespassing (vs. 4). Sin is in itself the agency of destruction. In old French, *le trépas* is both trespass and death. Job is guilty by association. According to the primitive notion of corporate personality, the guilt of the fathers is carried by the sons.

> The fathers have eaten sour grapes
> and the children's teeth are set on edge.

While Jeremiah (31:29-30) and Ezekiel (18:2) were attempting to abrogate the ancient adage in order to save their contemporaries from despair, Bildad used the principle it represented in order to indict the father for the crimes of his descendants. Dead men tell no tales, and the charge was easy. Possibly the speaker intended kindness toward the sufferer by suggesting that he did not charge him with a willful misdeed. He may also have insinuated that parents are responsible for juvenile delinquency. Another interpretation might be that, just as the sons had perished on account of secret faults, so also did Job endure the fruit of a hidden vice. In any case, the would-be comforter was now an accuser.

Divine injustice—clearly supposed by Job in chapters
6 and 7—is for Bildad an inconceivable blasphemy. He
thinks he can prove that God is just by the tradition of
the fathers. While Eliphaz had appealed in turn to his
observations, his private revelation and finally the careful investigations of his own academy or church, Bildad
quotes the wisdom of generations gone by (vss. 8-12).
Eliphaz claimed to be more than a lecturer: his authority stemmed from a prophetic sort of knowledge. Bildad
is different with his empirical information and he claims
no special inspiration. He is a humble man, indeed a
reverent agnostic, who acknowledges that

> we are but of yesterday and know nothing,
>   because our days upon earth are a shadow (vs. 9),

He seeks recourse in the lessons of history as distilled in
gnomic questions (vss. 11-12). The diagnosis and the
prescription reflect those of Eliphaz. Those who forget
God are cut off prematurely (vss. 12b-13a). The hypocrite (hānēph, vs. 13b) is in effect an apostate who re-
nounces his responsibility in life and his historical mission (Ps. 106:38; Isa. 10:6; Jer. 3:1; etc.). He cannot
hope to be spared. But let Job seek unto God and make
supplication to the Almighty (vs. 5), provided of course
that his moral purity backs up his prayer (vs. 6), a bewildering future lies open before him (vs. 7). God himself will "fill his mouth with laughter" (vs. 21), instead
of earth, no doubt, as Camus delicately said in *The Fall*.
    Bildad is insulated from the wormwood and the gall.
While history is the master of the present, it may never
be allowed to become its mistress. The lesson of the past
is always ambiguous; for the interpreter of history must
sift, stress and ignore. Of Justice Oliver Wendell

Holmes it was said, "A man whose presence carried tradition. And it was not oppressive but inspiring." A quarry is for building. True archaeology must lead to eschatology. Bildad demonstrates only that too often, as Frederic Prokosch put it,

> Man's enemy is his past,
> And the intellect, for ever more subtly arrayed,
> Is the secret, persuasive agent.

Tradition is less inherited than appropriated. The constant changing of the old order not only warns against the corrupting potency of a good custom, but it also cautions over

> The seeming truth which cunning time puts on
> To entrap the wisest.

Old Covenant Hebraism as well as New Covenant Christianity are erected upon the foundation of remembrance. But biblical memory is sacramental and creative, at Passover or Easter, as distinguished from institutional preservation in both synagogue and church. Bildad shows how the bulwark of tradition, a safeguard against the floods of experimentation, always turns into walls of a mausoleum.

III

"Thou Art the Man!"
First Discourse of Zophar, 11:1-20

The direct pointing of the finger by Nathan to King David was supported by facts. Likewise, prophetic condemnations of Israel and Judah testify to the law of justice in history. Even these, however, were not formu-

lated light-heartedly. The greater prophets attacked
their nation with reluctance and only under the violence
of inner compulsion. Respect for the mystery of the
human personality should restrain any counselor from
accusing in order to heal. In any case, prideless love and
awareness of solidarity in common guilt should lead the
friends to share rather than condemn. But Job's "reply"
to Bildad (chs. 9-10) convinced Zophar of the weakness
of his predecessors' circumlocutions. When his turn
comes, he merely pounces.

i

11:2.   Should not this master of words be answered?
      or should a man full of talk be justified?
3.   Should thy babble make men hold their peace?
      and when thou mockest, shall no man make
        thee ashamed?
4.   For thou hast said, My doctrine is pure,
      and I am clean in God's eyes.
5.   But oh that God could speak,
      and open his lips against thee;
6.   And that he should show thee the secrets of
      wisdom
      (for they disconcert human sagacity),
      Then, thou wouldest know that God pursueth[1]
      thee for thy guilt!

ii

7.   Canst thou by searching find out God?
      canst thou find out the Almighty unto
       perfection?[2]
8.   It is higher than heaven; what canst thou do?
      deeper than hell; what canst thou know?

---

[1] Hebrew obscure. Conjectural emendation of *yashsheh lekhâ* into *yish-chalekhâ.*

[2] Literally, "Canst thou discover the mystery of God,
     canst thou find the Almighty up to his limit?"

9. The measure thereof is longer than the earth,
       and broader than the sea.
10. If he sweep on and overflow,
       and want to rebuke, who can hinder him?
11. For he knoweth vain men;
       when he seeth evil, will he not then consider it?
12. Shall an empty man get a mind,
       or a wild ass' colt be born a man?

iii

13. As for thee, prepare thou to decide,
       and lift up thine hands to God.
14. If iniquity be in thine hand, put it far away,
       and let not wickedness dwell in thy tents.
15. For then shalt thou lift up thy face without spot;
       yea, thou shalt be steadfast, and shalt not fear:
16. Because thou shalt forget thy misery,
       and remember it as waters that pass away.
17. Life shall be clearer than the noonday
       and its darkness shall shine as a dawn.
18. And thou shalt be secure, because there is hope;
       yea, thou shalt dig in, and rest in safety.
19. Thou shalt lie down, and none shall make thee
       afraid;
       yea, many shall seek thy favors.[3]
20. But the eyes of the wicked shall fail,
       and they shall not escape,
       and their hope shall be as the giving up of the
       ghost.

At last the word of accusation has been bluntly spoken.
Against the patient's obstinate plea for the recognition of
his innocence, Zophar delivers the blow.

Know that God pursueth thee for thy guilt! (Vs. 6*b*.)

The poet reveals his art once more by keeping in reserve
the explicit formulation of a charge against Job himself

[3] Literally, "many shall caress thy face."

until the third speaker's turn came. He also reveals his
acquaintance with the common sin of professional the-
ologians by placing in the friends' mouths a dignified
mixture of truth and error. No caricature is intended.
The monotheistic creed of Zophar is at least as lofty as
that of his predecessors. His epistemological premises,
however, seem to go beyond theirs.

Eliphaz had appealed to empirical, pseudo-mystical
and institutional authority. Bildad had stood upon the
the treasury of popular wisdom. Zophar invokes an
esoteric wisdom which he denies to Job (vs. 6) but which
appears to be readily at his own disposal. He is a theologian of transcendence who correctly sees the futility
of man's natural ability to grasp the mystery of God.
Man's finiteness will obviously prevent him from study-
ing God as an object of scientific investigation. The
whole Bible agrees with Zophar on this point. Religion
as a quest is doomed to be pagan. It can be only a response
to an initial move, which is not man's. An Edomite
named Agur had "wearied himself about God but
failed" (Prov. 30:1 ff.). It is God who comes to the
garden when man still attempts to hide himself, and
cries, "Man, where art thou?" (Gen. 3:9.)

Zophar is right when he feels that only God can reveal
the "secret potency" of wisdom. Unfortunately, he too
easily claims for himself accessibility to such a revelation. The irony lies in the fact that, after his original
contribution on the beyondness of infinity, he has nothing more to say, but he says it with great charm. He plays
his own variations on the theme of the dependence of
man's happiness upon prayer and conduct. Piety and
morality, as for the satan of the popular story, are the
coins which purchase peace. If Job yielded to the ap-

peals of established religion, would he then fear God for nought?

IV

"Art Thou the First Adam?"

The Second Discourses of Eliphaz, 15:1-35; Bildad, 18:1-21; and Zophar, 20:1-29

As any dramatist whose genius is genuine enough to endure risks, the poet willfully becomes repetitious and dull for the sake of accuracy in psychological portrayal and local color. If his characters are tedious by turning in a vicious circle, the poet will not hesitate to bore his audience. The diagnosis of the patient's plight remains the same, "adversity is retribution for crime," and so also the prescription, "prayer changes things" (as the modern slogan has it, rather than "prayer changes persons") provided it is offered by a decent citizen of a decent community.

Because of the calculated repetition of the same motifs, it will not be necessary to analyze each strophe of every discourse of the friends. In the second round of discussion, the comforters are no longer attempting to comfort at all. They are not even making any progress in their effort to understand the cause of Job's adversity. But what they say, by reaction, contributes to the growth of Job's self-knowledge.

First of all, Eliphaz in his second discourse (ch. 15) falls back of course on his previously expressed reasoning on man's comparative unrighteousness (vss. 13-16); but before he comes to this favorite dogma of his, he offers an observation which is at once perceptive and revealing. It is perceptive, for it correctly describes, not the cause of the misfortunes which have struck a "perfect man," but the spiritual ailment which derives from those misfortunes. It is revealing, for it discloses the speaker's own insecurity.

15:4.   Yea, thou castest off fear,
         and restrainest prayer before God.
  5.   For thy guilt inspireth thy mouth,
         and thou choosest the tongue of the crafty.
  6.   Thine own mouth condemneth thee, and not I:
         yea, thine own lips testify against thee.

Job is not an ordinary criminal. He dares to defy the prevailing creed of the community. A nonconformist constitutes a threat to those who believe they think right but have never tested their thought in their own fire. "A heretic is he who has personal ideas," wrote Bossuet, quite unwittingly. Only a bold and living faith is secure enough to afford tolerance. Eliphaz shows the weakness of his own position by the violence of his verdict.

Thine own mouth condemneth thee, and not I (vs. 6a).

The poet conveys the paradox of a situation in which a sick man in agony reveals the health of his creative courage, while the superficially healthy representative of contentment and ease feels so uncomfortable that he loses control of his equilibrium. "What further need have we of witnesses?" ask all the high priests of history in self-defense before the "offensive" innocence of the "defendants" who face them (Matt. 26:65b).

Rolfe Humphries paid this tribute to Martha Carrier, hung as a witch in Salem in 1692:

> She faced the court, unloved, impolitic,
> With no defender but a shrewish tongue,
> Rude health, defiant nerve. To these, the sick
> Never show mercy.

Heretics, whom history may later prove right, are always wrong in their own days, for they unsettle the peace of weaklings around them. "You undermine religion with your threatening of God," translates James Moffatt (vs. 4).

In the second place, however, Eliphaz rightly discerns in Job a strain of defiance. He fears Job the heretic because he recognizes Job the Titan.

15:7.   Art thou the first man that was born?
             or wast thou brought forth before the hills?
    8.   Hast thou listened in the secret council of God?
             dost thou restrain wisdom to thyself?[1]
    9.   What knowest thou, that we know not?
             what understandest thou, which is not in us?
   10.   With us are both the grey-headed and very aged men,
             much elder than thy father.
   11.   Are the consolations of God too small for thee?
             or a word which is spoken to thee softly?

Eliphaz knows how relevant the myth of Adam is to all centuries. When Karl Barth was asked whether the serpent spoke to Eve in an audible voice, he laughed and remarked, "The serpent still speaks, does it not?" Eliphaz slyly suggests in verse 5, by using the expression

---

[1] I.e., "monopolize wisdom."

"the language of the crafty (*'arûm*)," that Job is now
eating the fruit of divine knowledge. The serpent is introduced in the ancient tale as the most crafty (*'ārûm*) of
all the creatures (Gen. 3:1). To court the godhead: this
is the meaning of original sin; not the inheritance of a
flaw through sexual transmission from generation to generation, but, in a far deeper sense, the sharing in all men
of the desire to force the limitations of manhood by becoming self-sufficient. Autonomy is practical atheism,
since a demand for self-vindication thereby rejects
grace. Eliphaz knows human nature well and he also
understands Job—but not himself.

Job usurps the status of divinity. He wishes to be like
God. To be sure, Eliphaz is not able to discern the
source of Joban defiance. It does not come from Job's
ambition to dominate the world by power. It emerges
from the depth of his sorrow. Nevertheless, the charge
does not altogether fall far from the mark. For Eliphaz
does not accuse Job of having brought upon himself his
misery by his attempts at self-deification while he was
still a prosperous man. He condemns the sufferer for
using grief as a fuel for pride. Therefore, Job's crime
is quite different from that of the tyrants of history, pro-
totypes of Lucifer, of whom it was said, as of the prince
of Tyre,

> Because thine heart is lifted up,
>   and thou hast said, I am God,
> I sit in the seat of the gods,
>   in the very heart of the seas;
> Yet thou art a man, and not God,
>   though thou claimest for thyself the
>   mind of a God! (Ezek. 28:2.)

The ancient Hebrews poetically personified divine wisdom as the sporting helper of the creator (Prov. 8:22-

31). Thus Michelangelo portrayed "her" on one of the Sistine frescoes as a slightly mischievous girl, holding an architect's plan (Prov. 8:30). While Wisdom may claim,

> Before the hills was I brought forth (Prov. 8:25*b*),

because she is a poetic face of divine creativity, Job has no right to forget the finiteness of his humanity. His opponent shows here a profound insight, and he exaggerates only a little when he says of the evil man,

> He stretched out his hand against God,
>   and strengthened himself against the
>   Almighty (Job 15:24),

literally, "he fancied himself to be a hero or a champion" braving omnipotence.

Like the first friend, Bildad displays his own anxiety. He fears that heroic defiance may bring about a retribution of cosmic proportions.

> Shall the earth be forsaken for thee?
>   or shall the rock be removed out of his
>   place? (18:4*bc*.)

And his dread may explain the vigor of his tone as he predicts the end of the evil man.

18:7.   His lusty steps shall be shortened.

.   .   .   .

13.   The First-Born of Death shall devour his
        strength.
14.   He shall be torn out of his tents in full security,
        and he will be dragged before the King of
        Terrors.

15.   Lilith[2] shall dwell in his tent
       they shall sprinkle with sulphur the place
       of his abode.

       .   .   .   .

17.   His remembrance shall perish from the earth,
       and he shall have no name in the street.
18.   He shall be driven from light into darkness,
       and chased out of the world.
19.   He shall have neither son nor nephew among
       his people,
       nor any survivor in the places of his sojourn.
20.   The West shall be astonished at his fate,
       and the East shall be affrighted.
21.   Surely, such is the destiny of an evil man;
       such is the lot of him that knoweth not God.

Cosmic in his ambition, the Titan will be chased out of
the "cosmos" (vs. 18), and the whole of mankind, occi-
dentals as well as orientals, will for a while be struck
with horror as they hear of his tragic end.

Zophar dutifully echoes the themes which Eliphaz
and Bildad are now playing upon. He too needs to
quell his nascent doubts (or at least "distraught
thoughts" 20:2). He therefore underlines the Prome-
thean fall:

20:6. Though his excellency mount up to the heavens,
       and his head reach unto the clouds;
7.   Yet he shall perish for ever like his own dung;
       they which have seen him shall say, Where
       is he?
8.   He shall fly away as a dream, and shall not be
       found:

2 Hebrew obscure. "Lilith" was a night demon haunting the Edomitic
wastes (Isa. 34:14).

yea, he shall be chased away as a vision in
the night.

.   .   .   .

11.   His bones are now full of youthful vigor,
but "she" will lie down with him in the dust.

.   .   .   .

15.   He hath swallowed down riches,
and he shall vomit them up again:
God shall cast them out of his belly.

16.   He shall suck the poison of asps:
the viper's tongue shall slay him.

A rather coarse language, which uncovers the extremity
to which anger mixed with fear may lead a man usually
engulfed in respectability. Those who began to speak
with therapeutic intent have been led to seek the victory
of their own brand of truth, and ultimately are reduced
to toying with irrelevance.

V

"Can a Man Be Profitable unto God?"

*The Third Discourses of Eliphaz, 22:1-30; Bildad,
25:1-6; 26:5-14; and Zophar [?],
24:18-24; 27:13-23*

Before the spectacle of sorrow, a judge has really nothing to say. If sympathy is the root of genius, religion
becomes sterile long before death, but it can still talk.
Instead of replying to Job's arguments which were
hurled at the dogma of retributive justice (ch. 21),

Eliphaz falls back upon his familiar creed, the creed to which he clings with the passion of desperation: divine transcendence. But his concern for the sovereignty of God is so completely divorced from a faith in God's love that he once again unfolds the theme of divine indifference (cf. 4:30).

22:2.   Can a man be profitable unto God,
          as he that is wise is profitable unto himself?
  3.   Is it any pleasure to the Almighty that thou art
          righteous?
          or is it gain for him that thou makest thy
          way perfect?

According to a certain form of theism, Eliphaz is right. God is not dependent upon man. He cannot profit from the deeds or the quality of a human being. But this form of theism is not that of the ancient Hebrews. The Bible always knows God to be the Absolute Sovereign and it is dreadfully aware of the abyss which splits human finiteness and corruption from divine infinity and goodness. But it also affirms that God is deeply and voluntarily involved in the affairs of human history and in the destiny of individuals as well as nations.

Eliphaz shows that a moralistic interpretation of religion is paradoxically related to a doctrine of theological impassiveness. A wise man is useful only to himself (Prov. 9:12). *A fortiori,* a man is useless to the Deity. In order to safeguard one aspect of the Being of God, Eliphaz is compelled to ignore the other. "As a bridegroom rejoiceth over the bride, so shall thy God rejoice over thee," sings the prophet (Isa. 62:5). The whole Bible is vibrant with the heartbeat of a God who looks down from heaven to wait for the sons of clay to respond.

As Rainer Maria Rilke saw it well in *Das Stundenbuch,* he is the God who says,

> *Ich bin, du Ängstlicher. Hörst du mich nicht*
> *mit allen meinen Sinnen an dir branden?*

> I am, thou anxious one. Dost thou not hear me rush to claim thee as the surf with all my mind and sense?

Throughout the pages of the Old Testament, the emotions of God are kindled together; and as his zeal overcomes his indignation, he submits to a passion for mankind. The New Testament brought to fruition, through its interpretation of Jesus as Christ, this inner core of Hebraic theology. Jesus, who knew that men at best are only "useless and unprofitable servants" (Luke 17:10), also declared in words and death, "Joy shall be in heaven over one sinner that repenteth" (Luke 15:7).

Critical reason may and should object that such a language is anthropopathic: it ascribes to the Deity human emotions. But it is the only language man can use. And biblical faith would not have arisen, had it not been a response to a God who, as Augustine later said, "is always calling aloud by cry, deed, death and destitution."

The concept of a passionless, unconcerned and immobile Godhead is foreign to Hebraism and Christianity, although it crept within Judaism and Christendom. On the face of it, a sublime theism affirms that God can do without man. In effect, such an affirmation represents a truncated truth, and any distortion leads to another. The cold dogmatist might have persisted in his earlier approach toward elucidating Job's predicament.

He might have pursued the motif of heroic defiance (cf. 15:1 ff.). He would then have gone a long way toward anticipating the hero's final discovery in the presence of the Lord, speaking from the whirlwind. A doctrinarian living in the past, however, is unable to move ahead. Eliphaz is forced to accuse Job once more (vss. 4-5). Perhaps inspired by Zophar's insinuations (20:17-27), he rakes his imagination, desperately trying to catalogue concretely a criminality susceptible of explaining the patient's plight. (He can do nothing better than make the grossest kind of blunder: he accuses Job of moral turpitude). So also ecclesiastical courts, from those who tried Joan of Arc to those who condemn Martin Luther and their modern successors.

6. For thou hast taken a pledge from thy brother for
        nought,
      and stripped the naked from their clothing.
7. Thou hast not given water to the weary to drink,
      and thou hast withholden bread from the hungry.
8. But as for the mighty man, he had the land;
      and the man of fame dwelt in it.
9. Thou hast sent widows away empty,
      and the arms of the fatherless have been broken.
      .   .   .   .
13. And thou sayest, How doth God know?
       can he judge through the dark cloud?[1]
14. Thick clouds are a covering to him, that he seeth
        not;
      and he walketh upon the vault of heaven.

Job indeed has attacked the dogma of divine omnis-cience (ch. 21), but not on account of his breaches of the

---

[1] The 'ărāphel represents a cultic motif of ancient Israel designed to sym-bolize the inscrutability and the unapproachability of God without negating his proximity (Exod. 20:18; I Kings 8:12; etc.).

moral law. To accuse him, however, of moral guilt enables Eliphaz to launch a final appeal, true to the approved techniques of Edomitic and other seminaries.

21. Reconcile thyself with God, and be at peace!
    thereby good shall come unto thee.
22. Receive, I pray thee, the law from his mouth,
    and lay up his words in thy heart.
23. If thou return to the Almighty with humility,[2]
    and put away iniquity far from thy tents,
24. If thou lay gold in the dust
    and the gold of Ophir among the stones of the
    brooks,[3]
25. Then the Almighty shall be thy treasure,
    and heaps of precious silver.
26. For then shalt thou have thy delight in the
    Almighty,
    and shalt lift up thy face unto God.
27. Thou shalt make thy prayer unto him,
    and he shall hear thee, and thou shalt pay thy
    vows.
28. For God abaseth the proud,
    and he shall save the humble.

Bildad lamely rehearses the familiar texts on man's insignificance, still showing his appreciation for great poetry.

25:4. How then can man be justified with God?
    or how can he be clean that is born of a woman?
5. Behold, even the moon shineth not
    and the stars are not pure in his sight.
6. How much less man that is a maggot,
    and the son of man, which is a worm?

Job himself must have been sensitive and appreciative

[2] Emending an obscure Hebrew text from the LXX.
[3] Probable rendering of a difficult text.

of Bildad's awareness of wonder before the holiness of
the creator:

26:5.   The Shades (Rephaim) tremble below,
          the waters'and the inhabitants thereof.
     6. Hades is naked before God
          and the lowest Hell hath no covering.
     7. He stretcheth out the north pole over the void
          and hangeth the earth upon "what-is-it?"

          .   .   .   .

    14. Lo, these are but the edges of his ways:
          how small a whisper do we hear of him?
         But the thunder of his power who can under-
              stand?

Zophar, if he spoke a third time, probably felt the irrelevance of this hymn. He therefore came again to the
point of brutality by insisting on the fate of the wicked
man (24:18-24; 27:13-23):

27:20.   Terrors take hold of him as flood waters,
          a whirlwind stealeth him away in the night.

The "friends" have fulfilled their mission. They have
upheld the creed valiantly and thus exhibited its failure
to cure a soul. If God and man remain external to one
another—if man is nothing more than a worm, and God
a distant, unmoved and immovable Being, an Absolute
which is detached from the giving and the seeking of
love—there is no hope, not even in a repentance, or in
the good deeds of behavior or piety. Prayer is just as
irrelevant as blasphemy.

   In spite of their lip service to the holiness of God, their
theism has become a form of idolatry. Self-appointed
speakers for God (15:11), they carry him in their breast-

pockets (12:6). They could not understand Job, for they
did not truly love God, hence did not truly love their
friend. He disturbed their security because he upset
their world view, and their fanaticism only shows the
uncertainty which gnawed at their hearts. As Paul Tillich expressed it in *The Courage to Be* (pp. 49-50),

Fanaticism . . . shows the anxiety which it was supposed to conquer, by attacking with disproportionate
violence those who disagree and who demonstrate by
their disagreement elements in the spiritual life of the
fanatic which he must suppress in himself. Because he
must suppress them in himself he must suppress them in
others. His anxiety forces him to persecute dissenters.

The affirmation of the Absolute has its legitimate
place—in the context of a rapport of communion. In
his recent autobiographical essay, *Surprised by Joy,*
C. S. Lewis concedes, "In the absolute . . . was 'the fuller
splendor' behind the 'sensuous curtain.' The emotion
that went with all this was certainly religious. But this
was a religion that cost nothing." And he added, "We
could talk religiously about the Absolute: but there was
no danger of Its doing anything to us." To believe in
God is not the same as to rely entirely and exclusively
upon him. Theism, for many of us, is not different from
Deism. We may acknowledge the existence and the su-
premacy of a Being we call God, but we keep him safely
and immovably outside of our decisions in daily living.
"It would never come 'here,' never (to be blunt) make
a nuisance of Itself." The faith of Job was not the belief
of his friends. This is the reason for which he was pursued by a reality which in his torture appeared like enmity. The friends, on the contrary, believed in a God
who respected the decency and the amenities of their ex-

istence. This is why they could believe in him. But "this quasi-religion was all one-way street; all *eros* . . . steaming up, but no *agape* darting down. There was nothing to fear; better still, nothing to obey. . . ." *Eros* toward God makes him indispensable, hence an idol. Only the acceptance of divine *agape* or self-giving love respects the freedom of God. Those who mistake for God their idea of the Absolute live, "like Dante's virtuous Pagans, 'in desire without hope.' Or like Spinoza they so love their God as to be unable even to wish that He should love them in return." Their concern for creedal correctness prevents them from looking at life itself.

It is the friends' intransigence which throws the hero back into his loneliness and compels him to go through the end of pain in destitution. But while the friends did not hear the Lord speak from the whirlwind, the rebel did, and that was the cause of his birth. Wrote Carlyle:

First must the dead Letter of Religion own itself dead, and drop piecemeal into dust, if the living Spirit of Religion, freed from this its charnel-house, is to arise on us, newborn of Heaven, and with new healing under its wings (*Sartor Resartus,* II, iii).

As Job knew all human help to be

The lion of Nothing,

he learned how to do without it. To his lips might be lent the words of Gloucester in *Henry VI,*

Shall I be flouted thus by dunghill grooms?

The function of an orthodoxy which has died is to spur heretics to lose hope in all human props, until they are prepared to receive grace alone.

Chapter 4

The Folly of a God-man

WHILE THE FRIENDS continue to intervene throughout the poetic "discussion," it is legitimate to let them fade out of the picture, as they indeed do when the poem reaches its climax at the Lord's speaking from the whirlwind. It is proposed now to follow the hero as he travels alone to the end of his night.

The fear and fascination of death which inspired his opening lament (ch. 3) persisted in his "reply" (chs. 6—7) to the first discourse of Eliphaz (chs. 4—5), but the sufferer's preoccupation with nothingness did not prevent him from grasping a hope. He discovered that the Enemy God was still concerned for him and even longed to find him (7:21). However, Job spoiled this hope by the perverse humor he displayed when he expected that his own death would frustrate the divine groping. He dared to imagine God confronting nothingness—the "Job-who-would-not-be"! Nevertheless, the thought transformed his outlook. It constitutes the first landmark, with a faint light upon the milestone, so to speak, along the route through darkness.

The contemplation of the void, with its horror and its attraction, is used by the poet as a device through which the hero acquires the knowledge of self. It indicates a stage toward salvation. The friends never concern themselves with the reality of the nought. This may be at once the cause and the symptom of their cowardice and spiritual sterility. Demetrios Capetanakis has remarked,

> Nothingness might save or destroy those who face it, but those who ignore it are condemned to irreality. They cannot pretend to a real life, which, if it is full of real risks, is also full of real promises.

Job looks at the prospect of nothingness with fear and yet without cowardice. He can even afford to jest about it, teasing a Deity with the same. By taking mortal risks, he makes an affirmation of life. In spite of his titanic determination to force the mystery of God, and perhaps because of it, the heretic becomes a prophet.

I

There Is No Mediator

Job's Reply to the First Discourse of Bildad, 9:1—10:21

Job seemingly ignores the meanness of the charge delivered by Bildad against his silenced children (8:4). According to the poet's rhetorical method of delayed reaction, already noted, Job appears to reply to the first discourse of Eliphaz (chs. 4—5). Soon, however, the

thought leaps abroad into the virgin ground of theological discovery, and Job stumbles upon one of the
momentous truths of the Bible: Man cannot purify himself; no human *pontifex maximus* can officiate on his behalf; no priest is able to cleanse him; no institution has
the power to intervene; man needs a mediator who
would be at once human and divine. Job discovers the
folly of hoping in a God-man. Nevertheless, his rejec-
tion of the idea uncovers his deepest craving.

The discourse is constituted by four poems of three
strophes each:

1. The Arbitrariness of God (9:2-13)
2. The Elusiveness of God (9:14-24)
3. The Inhumaneness of God (9:25—10:7)
4. The Creativeness of God (10:8-21)

Poem 1

The Arbitrariness of God, 9:2-13

i

9:2. I know it is so of a truth:
  but how should man be just with God?
 3. If one will contend with him,
  he cannot answer him one in a thousand times.
 4. However wise in heart, and mighty in strength,
  who hath hardened himself against him, and
  hath prospered?

ii

5. [God] removeth the mountains, and they know
  not,
  he overturneth them in his anger;
6. He shaketh the earth out of her place,
  and the pillars thereof tremble;

7. He commandeth the sun, and it riseth not:
    and sealeth up the stars;
8. He alone spreadeth out the heavens,
    and treadeth upon the waves of the sea.
9. He maketh the Bear and Orion,
    the Pleiades and the chambers of the south;
10. He doeth great things past finding out;
    yea, and wonders without number.

iii

11. Lo, he goeth by me, and I see him not:
    he passeth on also, but I perceive him not.
12. Behold, he taketh away, who can hinder him?
    who will say unto him, What doest thou?
13. God will not withdraw his anger,
    the helpers of Rahab do stoop under him.

Poem 2

The Elusiveness of God, 9:14-24

i

9:14. How much less shall I answer him,
       and choose out my words to reason with him?
15.   Who, though I were righteous, yet would not
       answer me,[1]
       when I make supplication for my acquittal.
16.   If I called, and he had answered me,
       yet would I not believe that he had harkened
       unto my voice.

ii

17.   For he breaketh me with a tempest,
       and multiplieth my wounds without cause.

---

[1] With the LXX and Syriac.

18. He will not suffer me to take my breath,
    and filleth me with bitterness.
19. If I speak of strength, lo, he is strong:
    and if of judgment, who shall set him[2] a time
        to plead?
20. If I justify myself, mine own mouth shall con-
        demn me;
    if I say, I am perfect, he shall prove me
        perverse.
21. I am perfect; I would risk my soul;
    I would despise my life.

iii

22. It is all one: therefore I say,
    he destroyeth the perfect and the wicked.
23. If the scourge slay suddenly,
    he will laugh at the trial of the innocent.
24. The earth is given into the hand of the wicked:
    he covereth the face of the judges thereof;
    if it is not he, who is it then?

Poem 3

The Inhumaneness of God, 9:25—10:7

i

9:25. Now my days are swifter than a courier:
    they flee away, they see no good.
26. They sweep by as the swift ships:
    as the eagle that hasteth to the prey.
27. If I say, I will forget my complaint,
    I will leave off my sad face, and smile;
28. I am afraid of all my sorrows,
    I know that thou wilt not hold me innocent.

[2] Text uncertain.

29.   I shall be found guilty;
     why then labor I in vain?

ii

30.   If I wash myself in snow water,
     and make my hands never so clean;
31.   Yet shalt thou plunge me in the ditch,
     and mine own clothes shall abhor me.
32.   For he is not a man, as I am, that I might answer
     him,
     that we should come together in judgment.
33.   Neither is there any daysman betwixt us,
     that might lay his hands upon us both.
34.   Let him take his rod away from me;
     and let not the dread of him terrify me:
35.   Then would I speak, and not fear him,
     for I am not guilty in mine own eyes.

iii

10:1.   Because I weary of my life,
     I will leave free rein to my complaint of him,[3]
2.   I will say unto God, Do not condemn me;
     show me wherefore thou contendest with me.
3.   Is it good unto thee that thou shouldest oppress,
     that thou shouldest despise the work of thine
     hands,
     and shine upon the counsel of the wicked?
4.   Hast thou eyes of flesh?
     or seest thou as man seeth?
5.   Are thy days as the days of mortal man?
     are thy years as a strong man's days,
6.   That thou inquirest after proofs of my guilt,
     and searchest after my sin?

[3] With the LXX.

7.   Thou knowest that I am not wicked;
        and there is none that can deliver out of thine
        hand.

Poem 4

The Creativeness of God, 10:8-21

i

10:8.   Thine hands have made me and fashioned me;
        afterwards thou dost turn about[4] and dost
        destroy me.
9.   Remember, I beseech thee, that thou hast made
        me as the clay;
        and wilt thou bring me into dust again?
10.   Hast thou not poured me out as milk,
        and curdled me like cheese?
11.   Thou hast clothed me with skin and flesh,
        and knit me together with bones and sinews.
12.   Thou hast granted me life and favor,
        and thy visitation hath preserved my spirit.

ii

13.   Yet these things hast thou hid in thine heart;
        I know that this was thy secret thought:
14.   If I sin, then thou markest me,
        and thou wilt not acquit me from mine
        iniquity.
15.   If I be wicked, woe is me;
        and if I be righteous, yet will I dare not lift up
        my head.
        I am sated with ignominy,
        and drunk with affliction.[5]

4 With the LXX and Syriac.
5 Probable rendering of a Hebrew word read only once (*hapax legomenon*)
in the Bible.

16. And if I lift myself up,[6] thou dost hunt me like a
     lion,
         and again work awful wonders upon me.
17. Thou renewest thine attacks[7] against me,
         and increasest thine indignation upon me;
         fresh hosts, a whole army, are against me.

iii

18. Wherefore then hast thou brought me forth out
     of the womb?
         oh that I had given up the ghost, and no eye
         had seen me!
19. I should have been as though I had not been;
         I should have been carried from the womb to
         the grave.
20. Are not my days few?
         Cease then, and let me alone, that I may
         brighten up a little,
21. Before I go whence I shall not return,
         even to the land of darkness and the deep
         shadow.

In these four poems which form an articulate whole,
Job moves forward under an initial appearance of retro-
gression. First, he appropriates the friends' lyricism on
the omnipotence of God, but his own experience of grief
leads him to pervert the idea of God's power into that of
God's arbitrariness. He borrows a hymnic sequence of
doxology (strophe *ii,* vss. 5-10) which presents itself in
Hebrew as a series of participial clauses of the litany
type. By embedding this canticle between strophe *i* (vss.
2-4) and strophe *iii* (vss. 11-13), he succeeds in twisting
its original intention, from praise to sarcasm. God can

---

[6] With Syriac.
[7] Reading the Hebrew word usually translated "witness" through its
Arabic cognate.

do all things, such is the creed of cultic adoration. Of course, he does, and without either control of inner standards or the check of outsiders. Job, ahead of Keats,

> ... saw too distinct into the core
> Of an eternal fierce destruction.

And thus Melville could castigate criminal behavior among his fellows by calling them "as unprincipled as the gods."

Eliphaz had said, "How should man be just with God?" (4:17). Job hastens to agree with him, adding at once that man does not have a chance (vs. 3). Any liturgical exaltation of the divine greatness (vss. 5-10) will only remind him of the brutality with which his own sons and daughters have been snatched (vs. 12). Bildad insinuated that they deserved their untimely end (8:4). Job merely remarks that when God takes away, man can neither hinder nor question (vs. 12). Any song (vs. 9) on the maker of the Pleiades and the Southern Cross (?) will only bring back his father-grief.

Since men cannot even ask God to give an account of himself (vs. 12*b*), the idea of the righteousness of God is placed in doubt. Job could have said, as Gloucester in *King Lear,*

> As flies to wanton boys are we to the gods;
> They kill us for their sport.

If God is not righteous, then the question of man's un-righteousness, as raised in *a fortiori* reasoning by Eliphaz and sardonically repeated by Job (vs. 2) be-comes irrelevant to the problem at hand. There is for

man no alternative to submission. Even the monsters of
the deep, which in the ancient myths of Semitic culture
were viewed as the "helpers" of personified Chaos, "do
stoop under" God (vs. 13). Job transforms the argument of Eliphaz by shifting the ground of the discussion
from the problem of guilt to that of finitude. Just as
God is not sovereign but arbitrary, man suffers not from
sin but from weakness. Eliphaz had claimed that men,
even divine beings, were impure before God (4:18, 5:1
ff.). Job retorts, in careful gradation, that mortal men
(vs. 2), not excepting the wise and the mighty among
them (vs. 4), and even the gods of the underworld (vs.
13) are impotent before God. The question, therefore,
is not one of ethical value but of relative strength.

Job will not submit to brute force, at least not silently.
The second poem (vss. 14-24) implies more than divine
arbitrariness: Is not God a coward that he eludes man's
questioning? Is it man who needs to be summoned to
the tribunal of the divine judge, or is it God who should
be compelled to appear before the court of man's critical
faculties? Centuries before the *Quatrains* of Omar
Khayyám raised with a sadness verging upon cynicism
the quest for the divine intent, men like Job threw back
their sorrow upon the responsibility of God, praying,

> For all the Sin wherewith the Face of Man
> Is blackened—Man's Forgiveness give—and take!

Virtue and vice are unrelated to man's fate (vs. 14).
The traditional gestures of piety are likewise useless in
producing happiness. Then, is Job starting to stagger
upon the meaning of pure religion? Not quite. At the
moment, he merely speculates in ignorance. Even if man

threw himself at the mercy of the judge and appealed
to God's "motherly grace" (for such is the undertone
of the verb used in vs. 15*b*), no trial would ever be held.
There is no answer to prayer (vs. 16). The thought of
divine caprice only exacerbates man's illusion of innocence through his awareness of ethical decency. Since
life is worthless (vs. 21), he may risk death by saying,
"God laughs at human torture" (vss. 22-24).

The third poem is linked directly to the transitional
motif, immediately preceding, as it depicts the inhuman-
ity of God (strophe *ii*, vss. 30-35). But while the friends
propose error in the midst of their truth, Job envisions
truth in the cloud of error and even blasphemy. Now
that his mood of defiance has subsided (strope *i*, vss. 25-
29), he is hurled back into the sea of his pain. He makes
it clear, however, that his tortures are more than physical. They are the torments of the spirit as well as of the
flesh. They are the peculiar symptoms of hell to a man
whose faith in a God of love has vanished. The torments
of the spirit may be more cruel than those of the flesh.
Cried Gerard Manley Hopkins, in his poem, "No
Worst, There Is None,"

O the mind, mind has mountains; cliffs of fall
Frightful, sheer, no-man-fathomed. Hold them cheap
May who ne'er hung there.

There is a limit to physical endurance, beyond which
pain itself is dulled. But not so in the realm of spiritual
agony, when man contemplates the abyss.

                    Nor does long our small
Durance deal with that steep or deep. Here! Creep,

Wretch, under a comfort serves in a whirlwind: all
Life death does end and each day dies with sleep.

The theological nature of Job's excruciation sends him
to the rim of martyrdom: he witnesses ahead of the centuries a truth which man's misery forces upon God. He
makes, even in a negative way, a plea for the Christian
mystery of the Incarnation.

Human morality and human ritual cannot render a
man pure, unless a God who cares for man's purity receives and welcomes within himself the vanity of human
achievements. But Job knows God only as an enemy.
He compares him to some drunken brute, an intoxicated
soldier on leave, who pushes the passer-by out of the
path into the ditch (vss. 30-31; cf. vs. 20). The vanity
of good works and of ritual absolution is here proclaimed, against the Protestant distortions of moralism
and the Catholic perversions of sacramentalism. Job's
experience is akin to that of some modern existentialists
who perceive that man is lost but do not know that God
is love.

Yet, the one-sidedness of Job's thought at this junc-
ture carries within it the seed of a stupendous truth. God
is inhuman because he is not man. If only God were
"emptied of his divinity" (Phil. 2:7), if only there were
a human God, then a dialogue between God and man
would become possible and a reconciliation could be
effected. The Hebrew text of verse 33 may be corrupt,
for some of the ancient versions read,

If only there were a daysman betwixt us!

The stress would then lie on the wistfulness of the wish
rather than on the abruptness of the denial. Either read-

ing, however, yields a similar idea. To reject a possibility is to show that it can be entertained—even only in a dream—and the fruit of the imagination, however remote within the realm of fancy, testifies to the vastness of man's need.

Job is not merely calling for a judge who would bring both God and man to trial, although the juridical picture is certainly in the background of his mind. He is not merely asking for a daysman or an arbiter who would make a decision—a thought which is also of a judicial nature. He is begging for a reconciliator, one who would place his hands on the shoulders of both God and man. One should imagine concretely the bold image (vs. 33) : God and man, now mutually estranged, who are no longer on speaking terms. A friend of both parties is needed who would be able and willing to act as an intermediary, a go-between, a mediator—someone who would have the confidence of both, someone who would participate in the realities in which both live. Job is craving for a God-man, who would create love between God and man, some Being "very God of very God" and "very man of very man" who by his own personality and life could achieve the rapprochement in the mutuality of trust. William Blake wrote in *The Divine Image*:

> For Mercy has a human heart,
> Pity, a human face;
> And Love, the human form divine;
> And Peace, the human dress.

To maintain that Job is predicting the advent of Christmas is of course not warranted by the text. The point, however, is that a prince of Hebraic monotheism is led by his agony to search so profoundly into the mystery of God that he does not hesitate to think in terms of

an interagent, at once divine and human, who would
represent man to God, in man's alienation, and mediate
God to man, in God's aloofness. Having rejected the
idea of a humanized Deity (vs. 32), no doubt because
he considered it as manifesting the folly of a deranged
mind, he now summons, even only for an instant, the
Being who would partake of holiness and infinity which
bespeak the divine realms and who would at the same
time sweat the sweat of blood and cry the tears of agony
which fit the finiteness of flesh. Job does not know, but
anticipates knowledge. T. S. Eliot writes in *The Dry
Salvages,*

> . . . These are only hints and guesses,
> Hints followed by guesses; and the rest
> Is prayer, observance, discipline, thought and action.
> The hint half-guessed, the gift half-understood, is
>   Incarnation.

Job is not in a state of defiance any longer. He wants love
on the cosmic level. While his reason murmurs heavenly
hatred, his faith of yesterday revives long enough to
force him into yearning for divine passion. The earlier
sarcasm about the God who laughs at the misery of the
innocent has made room for an obstinacy of demand
which will not give up until it is satisfied.

The daring of Job discloses a freedom similar to that
of many saints and mystics whose intimacy with infinity
gave them the right to irreverence. The story is told, for
instance, of Teresa of Avila who, having heard the plight
which had befallen the gardener of her convent, entered
her oratory burning with indignation. She prayed, "Is
it the way, Lord, you treat your friends?" To the reply,
"Is it not always the way I deal with my friends?" she

retorted, "Yes, Lord! I see why you have so few of them."

Job calls for love while he believes in hate. His arrogance is not that of the damned but that of the saints. Léon Bloy wrote to Barbey d'Aurévilly in 1873,

Since childhood I cannot remember a time when I did not suffer in all kinds of ways and often to an unbelievable degree. That simply proves that God loves me very much. I have meditated long and often on suffering. I am now convinced that nothing else is supernatural in this world. All the rest is human. . . .

Job is not yet ready to see a loving deity behind the persecutions which haunt him. His short-lived quest should not be confused with his ultimate readiness for a surrender to grace. He has not prayed with the psalmist of the *Kyrie eleison,* "Wash me and I shall be whiter than snow" (Ps. 51:7), but on the contrary he has declared, "If I wash myself with snow, yet shalt thou plunge me in the ditch" (vs. 31). He still wishes to be the author of his salvation. He cannot accept the services of a mediator, perhaps not so much because of the folly of a God-man, but rather because of the humiliation such a mediation would impose upon his sense of honor. Had there been any way for him to confront God face to face, he would only have pleaded for the recognition of his innocence (vs. 35b). Nevertheless, he has called for reconciliation. He has ventured into the theological unknown. He has dared to pioneer on the uncharted way. This poem stands as the second landmark in his voyage.

The last strophe of the third poem (10:1-7) returns to the thought of divine inhumaneness. But the purpose of comparing God to man is entirely different from the dream of a God-man. Job now questions the goodness of God by conjecturing divine finitude.

> Hast thou eyes of flesh?
> or seest thou as man seeth? (10:4.)

A moment ago, the sufferer had hoped that God might learn mercy from human example. Now he wonders whether God has not learned depravity from his imitation of man. But a new thought enters his mind as he asks,

> Is it good unto thee that thou shouldest oppress,
>   that thou shouldest despise the work of thine hands?
>   (Vs. 3ab.)

Thus the theme of divine creativeness provides him with a new basis for appeal. The fourth poem (10:8-21) dwells a while longer on the thought that God, the master artist who has sculpted man and breathed life into him, cannot abandon the creature of his hands. Even the Persian skeptic could write,

> And He that with his hand the Vessel made
> Will surely not in after Wrath destroy.

Creativeness means love; in Dante's words, it is

> *L'Amor che muove*
> *il sol e l'altre stelle.*

> Love that moves
> the sun and all the stars.

Man may be divorced from nature and from men, but he cannot be forgotten by his maker. Abraham Heschel

wrote in *Man Is Not Alone,* "The self can be distinctly
separated only at its branches; namely, from other individuals and other things but not at its roots." The hero
speaks nostalgically of the skill and genius with which
his heavenly progenitor formed him *in utero.* While a
psalmist of the Joban school, some years later, exclaims
at the wonder of his embryonic growth (Ps. 139:14 ff.),
the poet of Job stresses the tenderness and affection that
stem from aesthetic creativity. God cannot hate what he
makes. This thought, however, brings only brief solace.
Confronted by the present, the hero falls into a deeper
despair and strophe *iii* (10:18-19) resumes the initial
theme of the wish for non-being, while he immediately
adds, with a dying man's inconsistency familiar to all
mortals,

> Are not my days few? (10:20.)

The thwarting of the hope for a mediator is made the
more bitter by the irremediableness of death. In the next
discourse, the question must therefore be faced: could a
new life beyond the grave enable one to endure the life
of the present?

II

There Is No Resurrection

Job's Reply to the First Discourse of Zophar,
12:1—14:22

Now, at the conclusion of the first cycle of discussion,
Job prepares himself to answer the friends' plea for the
dogma of individual retribution. His own experience

leads him to reaffirm the thought of a ruthless uniformity in the rule of omnipotence (first poem, 12:2-25). Is a door still open to him? Only defiance which, because of the mortal risks it entails, will force—so he hopes—a meeting with God (second poem, 13:1-19). Death might offer a solution, but there is no resurrection of the dead (third poem, 13:20—14:22).

Poem 1
Experience versus Dogma, 12:2-25

i

12:2. No doubt but ye are the people,
    and wisdom shall die with you.
  3. But I have understanding as well as you;
    I am not inferior to you:
    yea: who knoweth not such things as these?
  4. I am as one mocked of his neighbor,
    who calleth upon God and God afflicteth him:[1]
    the just upright man is laughed to scorn.
  5. "Contempt for misfortune!" So thinketh the happy man;
    "A blow to him that is ready to slip with his feet!"
  6. The tents of robbers prosper,
    and they that provoke God are secure:
    they carry their god in their hand.

ii

  7. [You say:] "But ask now the beasts, and they shall teach thee;
    and the fowls of the air, and they shall tell thee:

---
[1] Hebrew obscure.

8. Or the plants of the earth, and they shall teach
   thee;
   or the fishes of the sea shall declare unto thee.
9. Who knoweth not among all these
   that the hand of the Lord hath wrought this,
10. In whose hand is the soul of every living thing,
   and the breath of all mankind?
11. Doth not the ear try words?
   ، and the mouth taste his meat?
12. With the ancient is wisdom,
   and in length of days understanding."

iii

13. [No!] With God is wisdom and strength,
   he hath counsel and understanding.
14. Behold, he breaketh down, and it cannot be
   built again:
   he shutteth up a man, and there can be no
   opening.
15. Behold, he withholdeth the waters, and they
   dry up:
   also, he sendeth them out, and they overturn
   the earth.
16. With him is strength and wisdom,
   the deceived and the deceiver are his.

17. He leadeth counselors away spoiled,
   and maketh the judges fools.
18. He looseth the bonds of kings,
   and he girdeth their loins with a girdle.
19. He leadeth princes away spoiled,
   and overthroweth the mighty.
20. He removeth away the speech of the trusty,
   and taketh away the understanding of the
   aged.

21. He poureth contempt upon princes,
    and weakeneth the strength of the tyrants.

22. He uncovereth the deeps out of darkness,
    and bringeth out to light the shadowy gloom.

23. He increaseth the nations and destroyeth them:
    he enlargeth the nations, and straiteneth them
    again.

24. He taketh away the mind of the chief of the
    people of the earth,
    and causeth them to wander in a trackless
    waste.

25. They grope in the dark without light,
    and he maketh them to stagger like a drunken
    man.

Poem 2

The Risk of Death, 13:1-19

i

13:1. Lo, mine eye hath seen all this,
    mine ear hath heard and understood it.

2. What ye know, the same do I know also:
    I am not inferior to you.

3. Surely, I would speak to the Almighty,
    and I desire to reason with God.

4. But ye are forgers of lies,
    ye are all physicians of no value.

5. Oh that ye would altogether hold your peace!
    and it should be your wisdom.

6. Hear now my reasoning,
    and hearken to the pleadings of my lips.

ii

7. Will ye speak falsely for God?
    and talk deceitfully for him?

8. Will ye be partial in his favor?
    will ye contend for God?
9. Would it be good that he should search you out?
    as one man mocketh another, do ye so mock
    him?
10. He will surely reprove you
    if in secret ye show partiality.
11. Shall not his excellency make you afraid?
    and his dread fall upon you?
12. Your proverbs of ashes are learned by rote;
    your defences are defences of clay.

iii

13. Hold your peace, let me alone, that I may speak,
    and let come on me what will.
14. Therefore shall I take my flesh in my teeth,
    and put my life in mine hand.
15. Behold, he will slay me, I have no hope;
    but I will maintain mine own ways before
    him.
16. This might even be my salvation:
    for a hypocrite shall not come before him.
17. Hear diligently my speech,
    and my declaration with your ears.
18. Behold now, I have ordered my cause;
    I know that I shall be justified.
19. Who is he that will plead with me?
    For then I would hold my tongue and give
    up the ghost.

Poem 3
Prayer for Life Eternal, 13:20—14:22

i

13:20. Only two things do not withhold from me;
    then will I not hide myself from thee.

21. Withdraw thine hand far from me:
    and let not thy dread make me afraid.
22. Then call thou, and I will answer:
    or let me speak, and answer thou me.
23. How many are mine iniquities and sins?
    make me to know my transgression and my
    sin.
24. Wherefore hidest thou thy face,
    and holdest me for thine enemy?
25. Wilt thou break a leaf driven to and fro?
    and wilt thou pursue the dry stubble?
26. For thou writest bitter things against me,
    and makest me to inherit the iniquities of my
    youth.
27. Thou puttest my feet also in the stocks,
    and lookest narrowly unto all my paths;
    thou settest a print upon the heels of my feet.

ii

28. As a rotten thing consumeth,
    or as a garment that is moth-eaten,
14:1. Man that is born of a woman
    is of a few days, and full of trouble.
2. He cometh forth like a flower,
    and is cut down:
    He fleeth also as a shadow,
    and continueth not.
3. And dost thou open thine eyes upon such a one,
    and bringest me into judgment with thee?
4. Who can bring a clean thing out of an unclean?
    not one.
5. Seeing his days are determined,
    the number of his months are with thee,
    thou hast appointed his bounds that he can-
    not pass;

6.   Turn from him and desist from him,
      that he may enjoy, as a hireling, his day.

iii

7.   For there is hope for a tree,
      if it be cut down, that it will sprout again,
      and that the tender branch thereof will not
         cease.

8.   Though the root thereof wax old in the earth,
      and the stock thereof die in the ground;

9.   Yet through the scent of water it will bud,
      and bring forth boughs like a plant.

10.   But man dieth, and wasteth away:
      yea, man giveth up the ghost, and where is he?

11.   As the waters fail from an inland sea,
      and the flood decayeth and drieth up;

12.   So man lieth down, and riseth not:
      till the heavens be no more, they shall not
         awake,
      nor be raised out of their sleep.

iv

13.   Oh that thou wouldest hide me in the grave,
      that thou wouldest keep me secret, until thy
         wrath be past,
      that thou wouldest appoint me a set time, and
         remember me!

14.   If a man die, shall he live again?
      all the days of mine appointed time will I
         wait, till my relief come.

15.   Thou shalt call, and I will answer thee:
      thou wilt have a desire for the work of thine
         hands.

16.   Whereas now thou numberest my steps,
      then thou wouldest not watch over my sin.

17.   Now, my transgression is sealed up in a bag,
          and thou sewest up mine iniquity.

                                  v

18.   And surely the mountain falling cometh to
          crumbling,
          and the rock is removed out of his place.
19.   The waters wear the stones:
          the torrents wash away the soil of the earth;
          so thou destroyest the hope of man.
20.   Thou prevailest for ever against him, and he
          passeth:
          thou changest his countenance, and sendest
          him away.
21.   His sons come to honor, and he knoweth it not;
          and they are brought low, but he perceiveth
          it not.
22.   Only for himself in his flesh he suffereth,
          and in his soul for himself he waileth.

Now that the three representatives of the wisdom
community have had their say, Job is completely aware
of his ostracism. The gulf between him and his oppo-
nents is so wide that no understanding will ever be possible. He therefore begins the first poem of his reply
(12:2-25) to Zophar's first discourse (ch. 11) with a
mild sarcasm which covers bitterness and assurance at
the same time:

                No doubt but ye are the people,
                    and wisdom shall die with you (12:2).

Not only in the so-called "democratic" periods of history is the *vox populi* identified with the *vox Dei*. Orthodoxy is "the right opinion" only when the majority
dictates. A solitary nonconformist may well be "a laugh-

ing stock to his neighbor" (vs. 4a), but later generations
may prove him to be "right."

> In a world of fugitives
> The person taking the opposite direction
> Will appear to run away,

says T. S. Eliot in *The Family Reunion*. Those who
claim the last word in wisdom (vs. 2b) are usually those
who bring up the rear but hardly ever show the way. Job
may appear to be an eccentric, "so extravagant that a
discreet poet would not venture to set [him] upon the
stage" (Lord Chesterfield), but he reveals an authority
of his own when he shouts his orthodoxy. Of course,
he has prayed to God, and God in answer to prayer has
afflicted him (vs. 4b). According to the popular men-
tality of the time—and of other times—fate is always
deserved; hence it constitutes an index of inner criminality (vs. 5). But experience shows too often the prosperity of evil (vs. 6a). Many successful men use religion
as a technique for their success, and the god they worship
is a manufactured idol: "They carry their god in their
hand" (vs. 6b).

The traditional wisdom on God's power, Job accepts
(vss. 7-11), although he appeals from the authority of
the elders (vs. 12) to the knowledge which is God's
(vs. 13). As much as the friends, he admits the divine
omnipotence (vss. 13-16). The sequence of participial
phrases he uses (vss. 17-21 and 22-25) in the original
Hebrew suggests once more that he is quoting a familiar
hymn (cf. 9:5-10). He does so probably in order to
establish his own adherence to the dogma. This allows
him to say in the second poem (13:1-19) that his standing is in no way inferior to that of his entourage (vss.

1-6). But he gives up the attempt to convince "forgers of lies" and "physicians of no value" (vs. 4). Their authority is exterior and superficial (vss. 7-12). It is now with God alone that he will contend (vss. 13-19). Once more the mood is that of titanic defiance. Melville lends these words to Ahab, addressing the fire:

No fearless fool now fronts thee. I own thy speechless power; but to the last gasp of my earthquake life will dispute its unconditional, unintegral mastery in me. In the midst of the personified impersonal, a personality stands here.

Not that Job is exempt from the dread of God. Indeed, he is somewhat astonished by the fact that the friends are those who talk as if they were not in awe of the Deity (vs. 11). What he is going to say will, however, truly horrify them. He requests special attention, thereby announcing the excessive tone of his forthcoming declaration (vs. 13). Taking his flesh in his teeth, or putting his life in his hand (vs. 14), he is bold enough to say,

Behold, God will slay me, I have no hope;
    but I will maintain mine own ways before him (vs. 15).

The King James Version and many other translations render this verse in the sublime and familiar words,

Though he slay me, yet will I trust in him.

Unfortunately, this phrase represents a hallowed mistranslation, suggested by a pious correction of the scribes in the margin of the Hebrew manuscripts. The text

reads *lō'*, "not," rather than *lô*, "to him." Traditional
translators have further assented to the wishful thinking
of the scribes: they have rendered the Hebrew verb "to
wait" or "to hope" by "to trust" and introduced the re-
strictive adverb "yet" as a link of thought, although it
is absent in the original, in both text and marginal notes.
Finally, they have done all this in complete disregard of
Job's temper as it is revealed by the whole chapter, of
the warnings that he was going to make a shocking pro-
nouncement (vs. 14) and especially of the outburst of
arrogance which is immediately following.

but I will maintain mine own ways before him (vs. 15*b*).

While some modern readers feel disappointed at losing
this declaration of "faith at all costs," or of "faith nevertheless," of devotion without condition, of love most
self-giving, the rigors of scientific honesty must of
course be observed. In fact, the correct translation represents a gain rather than a loss. Job is the slave of truth:
he is willing to die for it, and while his service to the
hardest mistress entails the self-assertion of pride, it
becomes also a basis for hope. God cannot fail to be
impressed by the heroism of sincerity.

This might even be my salvation:
    for a hypocrite shall not come before him (vs. 16).

Unconsciously, Job pays tribute to the divinity of God.
After having accused him of arbitrariness, he still trusts
divine love.
    The third poem implies this trust more clearly as the
hero now turns to the style of direct address in prayer

(13:20—14:17). Like the mysterious "K." in Kafka's
The Trial, Job suspects that charges are made against
him, but his torment lies precisely in his ignorance of
the specific charges (vs. 23). The hostility of God is
beyond his comprehension. His dread (vs. 21) does not
prevent his humor, however. He may be punning on his
own name when he asks the Deity,

Why...holdest [thou] me for thine enemy? (Vs. 24*b*.)

The name "Job" (*'iyyôbh*) is probably derived from the
same root as the word "enemy" (*'ôyēbh*). In this poem,
Job is no longer in the mood of defiance. He adopts the
language of the love dialogue transposed theologically
from the human emotion of romantic attraction. Like
Hosea, other prophets, and several psalmists, Job unconsciously compares the God-man rapport to the love
of man and woman; but unlike the Jewish, Moslem and
Christian mystics of later ages, biblical men who have
known intimacy with the divine never use an erotic terminology in a pantheistic sense of loss of the self in the
divine whole through spiritual identification. Indeed,
Job as well as any other poet or thinker of the Bible
stresses the sharp distinction that separates human finitude from divine infinity; and while the union is com-
parable to a marriage of exquisite tenderness, it never
eradicates the consciousness of object-subject relation-
ship.

Then call thou, and I will respond (vs. 22*a*).

The wane of the previous attitude of insolence also appears in the lyricism of the strains on man's mortality,

> For there is hope for a tree (vs. 7*a*):
> But man dieth and wasteth away (vs. 10*a*),

and in the poetic "reprise" in the interrogative mood,

> If a man die, shall he live again? (Vs. 14*a*.)

This theme is intertwined with the motif of the love dialogue:

> Oh that thou wouldest appoint me "a date" and remember me! (Vs. 13*c*.)

Once again, with the insistence of human lovers:

> Thou shalt call, and I will respond to thee (vs. 15*a*).

The romantic imagery persists under the repetition of the motif of creatureliness, with its aesthetic overtones,

> Thou wilt have a desire for the work of thine hands (vs. 15*b*),

literally, "thou wilt pale with the passion of desire," or possibly even "faint from delayed waiting."

As in the Old Testament generally, and in the Psalms in particular, death is not to be slurred over as a pleasant ushering into eternal delight. Immortality of the soul by natural right is an unbiblical fancy. A biblical man prays for life eternal and finally affirms his hope in it, but he does so while fully aware of the finality of natural life and its annihilation. Job is not yet believing that God will raise him from the dead. On the contrary, he is denying the Egyptian belief in resurrection. The poet is aware of the slowness of psychological maturation and withholds Job's affirmation until a later stage of the hero's growth (19:25-26). Nevertheless, the thought of a rapport after death, initiated and effected by the creator of life, has entered the mind of the distraught searcher.

It will be observed, however, that Job's idea of life eternal, so briefly entertained in this poem, is not based upon a philosophical need of retribution in the "hereafter" for want of a retribution in the "here-and-now." Job, of all men, did not think up this so-called "proof" of immortality! If Job had affirmed the expectation of life eternal as a reward for his persistence in integrity upon earth, he would have answered the whole question of the satan (1:9) by a pitiable defeat. In defying God, Job is faithful to God. In refusing to repent, even for the hope of an eternal recompense, Job is serving God gratuitously. His arrogance is paradoxically the sign of his fidelity. His denial of the belief in the resurrection is the *sine qua non* of his faith.

The pathos of the last strophe (vss. 13-17) is made the more gripping by the fact that Job has already said, in the immediately preceding couplet,

So man lieth down and riseth not (vs. 12*a*).

There is a French folk saying that is not without humorous understatement: *Quand on meurt, c'est pour longtemps,* "When one dies, it's for a long time." Job toys with the idea of a rebirth, but he is too much a theologian of Hebraism to accept the attractiveness of illusory pagan mythology. He knows that man does not rise from the dead—that is to say, through human techniques or natural rights—and he conveys the nausea of the feeling of extinction as well as the depth of his despair by adding,

till the heavens be no more, they shall not awake, nor be raised out of their sleep (vs. 12 *bc*).

Yet, the flaming-up of his certainty in God's love makes him continue with strophe *iv* (vss. 13-17).

Thou wilt have desire for the work of thine hands (vs. 15*b*).

When biblical man breaks up the age-long resistance of Hebraism to the mythological phantasmagory of Egypt, he does so neither on the ground of man's right through the natural immortality of his soul nor on the ground of man's need for retributive justice beyond the grave, but only because of his awareness of a communion with God who is the creator of the universe and of him (cf. 19:25-26 and the prayer of the Joban school, Ps. 73:23-26).[2]

How far Job has progressed from his earlier fearful "flirtation" with nothingness is now apparent. He is not yet in a position to declare, "I know that my redeemer liveth" (19:25*a*), but he is no longer wishing he were as one who would not be. The haunting melody of Omar Khayyám, which was not inappropriate as an illustration of the initial lament of Job (ch. 3) and of the reply to the first discourse of Eliphaz (chs. 6—7), would now be incongruous. One may discern the distance which separates Job from the inane beauty of the quatrain:

A Moment's Halt—a momentary taste
Of Being from the Well amid the Waste—

[2] See Terrien, *The Psalms* . . . , p. 259.

> And Lo!—the phantom Caravan has reach'd
> The Nothing it set out from—Oh, make haste!

Far from being attracted by nothingness, Job is now entertaining the dream of being called or summoned from the underworld for a tryst with the maker of existence. The modern echo is equally ill-fitting. In the poem, "And Death Shall Have No Dominion," Dylan Thomas utters his dread of an unknown which has no room for divine presence:

> And you, my father, there on the sad height,
> Curse, bless, me now with your fierce tears, I pray.
> Do not go gentle into that good night.
> Rage, rage against the dying of the light.

God may still be the enemy of Job (14:16-17), but Job lives in the world of God and sees more and more clearly beyond this enmity.

Chapter 5

The Need for a Christ

IN THE FIRST cycle of discussion (chs. 3—14), the hero has maintained his innocence and concluded by affirming his hope that he might have access to the divine presence. But his pride was unabated, for his last word on this theme was,

I know that I shall be justified (13:18*b*).

In the second cycle of discussion (chs. 15—21), however, he overcomes in some limited way his desire for self-justification by developing the expectation of a heavenly witness (ch. 16).

The motif on the folly of a God-man, leading to the denial of a mediator (ch. 9), now reappears in the theme of the heavenly advocate (ch. 16) and of the redeemer (ch. 19). At the same time, by a remarkable intermingling of thought, the denial of a belief in the resurrection (ch. 14) makes room—simultaneously with the

appearance of the redeemer motif—for the affirmation
of a vision of God after death (ch. 19).

I

"My Witness Is in Heaven"

Job's Reply to the Second Discourse of Eliphaz,
16:2—17:16

i

16:2.   I have heard many such things:
      miserable comforters are ye all.
  3.   [You say:] Shall vain words have an end?
      or what emboldeneth thee that thou answerest?
  4.   I also could speak as ye do:
      if your soul were in my soul's stead,
  I could heap up words against you,
      and shake mine head at you.
  5.   But I would strengthen you with my mouth,
      and the moving of my lips should assuage your
        grief.
  6.   Though I speak, my grief remaineth,
      and if I desist, doth it depart from me?

ii

  7.   Now, alas, God hath exhausted me:
      he hath made desolate all my company.[1]
  8.   [Misfortune] hath seized me and witnesseth
        against me;[1]
      my leanness beareth testimony to my face.
  9.   He teareth me in his wrath, who hateth me:
      he gnasheth upon me with his teeth;
      mine enemy sharpeneth his eyes upon me.

[1] Hebrew uncertain.

10. They have gaped upon me with their mouth;
    they have smitten me upon the cheek reproach-
       fully;
    they have gathered themselves together against
      me.
11. God hath delivered me to the ungodly,
    and turned me over into the hands of the
      wicked.

iii

12. I was at ease, but he hath broken me asunder:
    he hath also taken me by my neck, and shaken
      me to pieces,
    and set me up for his mark.
13. His archers compass me round about,
    he cleaveth my reins asunder, and doth not
      spare;
    he poureth out my gall upon the ground.
14. He breaketh me with breach upon breach;
    he runneth upon me like a giant.
15. I have sewed sackcloth upon my skin,
    and defiled my horn in the dust.
16. My face is foul with weeping,
    and on my eyelids is the shadow of death;
17. Not for any injustice in mine hands:
    also my prayer is pure.

iv

18. O earth, cover not thou my blood,
    and let my cry have no resting place!
19. Even now, behold, my witness is in heaven,
    and mine advocate is on high.
20. (My cries are my intercessors,[2]
    mine eye poureth tears unto God.)
21. Oh that he would plead for man with God
    as a man pleadeth for his neighbor!

[2] Hebrew obscure.

22. When a few years are come,
    then I shall go to the place whence I shall not
    return.

v

17:1. My spirit is deranged,
      my days are extinct,
      the graveyard is waiting for me.
2. Are there not mockers with me?
   and doth not mine eye spend the night awake
   in their provocation?
3. Lay down a pledge for me with thyself!
   who is he that will give surety for me?
4. For thou hast hid their heart from understanding:
   therefore no one lifteth up his hand.[3]
5. As one inviteth friends to partake [of his
   wealth]
   while the eyes of his own sons languish.

vi

6. He hath made me also a byword of the nations;
   someone upon whose face people spit I have
   become.
7. Mine eye also is dim by reason of sorrow,
   and my limbs vanish as a shadow.[3]
8. Upright men shall be astonished at this,
   and the innocent man shall stir up himself
   against the hypocrite.
9. The righteous also shall hold on his way,
   and he that hath clean hands shall be stronger
   and stronger.
10. But as for you all, do ye return, and come now:
    I shall not find one wise man among you.

vii

11. My days are past, my purposes are broken off,
    even the thoughts of mine heart.

[3] Hebrew uncertain.

12. [You say:] The night will soon be day;
    the light is near to the present gloom.
13. [No!] if I hope, it is that hell be my house;
    I have spread my bed in the dark abode;
14. To the pit I cry, Thou art my father,
    and to the worms, My mother and my sister.
15. Where then is now my hope?
    and my happiness,[4] who shall see it?
16. Shall they go down with me to the gates of hell?
    shall we find our rest together in the dust?[5]

Pierced by the resumption of the charges which Eliphaz makes in his second discourse (ch. 15), Job reacts at once:

Miserable comforters are ye all (16:2*b*).

Irony rules his tone. If his friends could take his place and he were their comforter, he could talk just as they do and even shake his head in the gesture of commiseration (vss. 4-6). But his grief is beyond their understanding (vss. 7-11). God pursues him relentlessly, as a champion in a fight.

He breaketh me with breach upon breach,
he runneth upon me like a giant (vs. 14).

Through the use of onomatopoeia, the Hebrew suggests the sounds of a mortal combat: *"Yphretsēnî phérets 'al penê-phárets, yārûts 'alây keyhibbôr."* God and Job have reached a deadlock, but man will not yield, still claiming,

My prayer is pure (vs. 17*b*).

It is the heroism of Job which at once creates his arrogance and yet makes him the champion of aching man-

---

[4] With the LXX.
[5] Hebrew uncertain.

kind. Kierkegaard, among others, has shown how Job
can truly represent man:

Job! Job! Job! Didst thou indeed utter nothing but
these beautiful words, "The Lord gave, the Lord hath
taken away, blessed be the name of the Lord"? Didst
thou say nothing more? In all thy distress didst thou
merely continue to repeat these words? Why wast thou
silent for seven days and nights? What went on in thy
soul? When the whole world fell to pieces above thy
head and lay in potsherds around thee, didst thou at once
possess this superhuman composure, didst thou at once
have love's interpretation and the frank-heartedness of
confidence and faith? Is thy door then closed against
the afflicted man, can he expect from thee no other relief
than that pitiable consolation which worldly wisdom
offers by reciting a paragraph about the perfection of
life? Hast thou nothing more to say? Dost thou not
dare to say more than what the false comforters lacon-
ically mete out to the individual, what the false comforters, rigid as a master of ceremony, prescribe to the
individual, that in the hour of distress it is seemly to
say, "The Lord gave, the Lord hath taken away, blessed
be the name of the Lord"—neither more nor less, just
as one says "Prosit" when a person sneezes! No, thou
who . . . wast a sword for the oppressed, a cudgel to
protect the old, a staff for the decrepit, thou didst not fail
men when all was riven asunder—then thou wast a
mouth for the afflicted, and a cry for the contrite, and a
shriek for the anguished, and an assuagement for all who
were rendered dumb by torments, a faithful witness to
the distress and grief a heart can harbor, a trustworthy
advocate who dared to complain "in anguish of spirit"
and to contend with God. (*Repetition*.)

What gives the struggle its full meaning is that Job,
although he expects death at the hands of God himself,

will not even give up *after he dies.* Any ancient Semite,
victim of murder, could be confident that one of his
survivors among his descendants or close relatives, like
his sons, his nephews, his brothers or his cousins, would
seek his murderer out and "buy back" or "redeem" his
honor. To redeem the blood of a victim was elemental
duty.

One of the stories of the pre-Islamic Arabs tells of a
youth whose father had been killed by a ruffian of colos-
sal stature. The boy was frightened at the prospect of
engaging such an adversary in obviously unequal conditions. Plagued by doubt, he consulted an idol by the
mantic device of shooting arrows at its statue while asking, "Should I avenge my father?" Three times he received the same answer: "Don't do it." But the knowledge of his duty as the redeemer of his progenitor over-
came his doubts as well as his dread of death. He threw
his bow at the idol, saying, "You would not give so cowardly an advice, had your own father been slain!" He
went, and avenged.

Job has no human avenger. He does not yet come to
the knowledge that he has one in heaven (19:25). But
he suddenly discovers that someone will defend him
after he dies. That the thought of the avenging of his
own blood has reached the threshold of his consciousness is clear from the call,

> O earth, cover not thou my blood,
>   and let my cry have no resting place! (Vs. 18.)

According to animistic beliefs, the blood spilled in
murder cries out for vengeance (Gen. 4:10-11) until it
is covered by dust (Ezek. 24:7). Personified earth is

summoned to his side. Soon he leaps upon a new certainty:

> Even now, behold, my witness is in heaven,
> and mine advocate is on high (vs. 19).

Many commentators have maintained that this mysterious figure is none other than that of God himself.
They believe that Job is appealing "from God to God."
According to this view, Job perceives within the divine
personality a tension between hate and love, and while
he knows that God is going to kill him off, he thinks
that the same God is also ready to testify on his behalf.
In this connection, exegetes are prone to quote the lines
of Tennyson's "Despair":

> Ah, yet—I have had some glimmer, at times, in my
>   gloomiest woe,
> Of a God behind all—after all—the great God, for
>   aught that I know;
> But the God of love and of hell together—they cannot
>   be thought,
> If there be such a God, may the Great God curse him
>   and bring him to nought!

It is correct to assume that Job's conception of the Deity
involves a contradiction between hostility and benevolence (cf. 7:21; 10:9 ff.; 13:16; 14:13 ff.). Nevertheless,
the common interpretation of this passage disregards the
preceding as well as the following context. The defend-
ing witness cannot be God, for God is already the prose-

cuting agent (vss. 12-14). The witness cannot be God
for Job adds,

> Oh that he would plead for man with God,
>   as a man pleadeth for his neighbor! (Vs. 21.)

The intervening parenthesis (vs. 20), the text of which
has most probably been corrupted in manuscript transmission, does not provide either support or objection to
the thesis here held. In fact, Job has already called for
a mediator (9:33) who would bring God and man together in a friendly exchange. The theme of the mediator now reappears in modified form. Job is certain that
a heavenly being will defend him at the court of God.

At the same time, Job is no longer claiming access to
self-cleansing or justification (9:30; 13:18b). He is
yielding to the services of another. He is engaged on the
path to surrender of the self.

To be sure, the one who will vouch for him is still an
advocate of his pride. He will "maintain" his human
rights before God. The language is still that of the court
of law. Job has not yet given up his sense of honor and
the riches of his integrity. His virtue remains his last
possession. It is the last obstacle between him and the
vision of God.

In the meantime, no man around him will "lift up his
hand" to offer a pledge of his decency (17:3-4). He
therefore relapses into his complaint, looking for the
grave (vss. 11 ff.). At least, he refuses illusions (vs. 12).
The love motif that he used at the end of his prayer for
eternal life (14:13 ff.) to describe his dream of a gracious God, is now once more before him, but he applies
it perversely to death itself. He has already spread his

couch in darkness (vs. 13*b*; cf. Ps. 139:8*b*), and he calls
the worms, "My mother and my sister" (vs. 14*b*). But
there is also another kind of marriage. "In the depth of
the abyss," writes Miguel de Unamuno in *The Tragic
Sense of Life,* "the despair of the heart and of the will
and the scepticism of reason meet face to face and embrace like brothers. . . . It is from this embrace, a tragic
—that is to say, an intimately loving—embrace, that the
wellspring of life will flow, a life serious and terrible."
It can already be seen that the poem of Job is not a treatise on the problem of undeserved suffering. It uses suffering as a way of isolating man from society, from God
and from himself, in order to place him in the situation
of creatureliness fulfilled.

II

"I Know My Redeemer Liveth"

*Job's Reply to the Second Discourse of Bildad,
19:1-29*

i

19:2.   How long will ye vex my soul?
      and break me in pieces with words?
  3.   These ten times have ye reproached me:
      are ye not ashamed to oppress me?[1]
  4.   And be it indeed that I have erred,
      mine error remaineth with myself.
  5.   If indeed ye will magnify yourselves against me,
      and plead against me my reproach;

1 With the LXX.

6.   Know then that God hath perverted my cause,
     and hath compassed me with his net.

ii

7.   Behold, I cry out of wrong, but I am not heard:
     I cry aloud, but there is no justice.
8.   He hath fenced up my way, that I cannot pass,
     and he hath set darkness in my paths.
9.   He hath stripped me of my glory,
     and taken the crown from mine head.
10.   He hath destroyed me on every side, and I am
     gone:
     and mine hope hath he removed like a tree.
11.   He hath also kindled his wrath against me,
     and he counteth me unto him as his enemy.
12.   His troops of raiders come together,
     and raise up their way against me,
     and encamp round about my tent.

iii

13.   My brethren have become distant from me,
     and mine acquaintances are verily estranged
     from me.
14.   My kinsfolk have failed me,
     and my familiar friends have forgotten me.
15.   Even the guests of mine house, and my maids,
     they count me for a stranger:
     I am an alien in their sight.
16.   To my own slave I call, and he giveth no answer,
     although I entreat him with my mouth.
17.   My breath is strange to my wife,
     I am loathsome to the sons of my mother.
18.   Yea, even urchins despise me:
     I arise and they speak against me.

19.   All my inward friends abhor me:
         and they whom I love are turned against me.

iv

20.   My bone cleaveth to my skin and to my flesh,
         and I am escaped with the skin of my teeth.
21.   Have pity upon me, have pity upon me, O ye my
            friends;
         for the hand of God hath touched me.
22.   Why do ye persecute me as God,
         and are not sated with my flesh?
23.   Oh that my words were now written!
         Oh that they were engraved on a scroll of
            brass!
24.   Oh that with an iron pen and lead
         they were graven in the rock for ever!

v

25.   But as for me, I know that my redeemer liveth,
         and that he shall arise at the latter day upon
            the dust;
26.   And after I wake up, I shall stand up,[2]
         and from within my flesh shall I see God;
27.   Whom I, even I, shall see for myself,
         and mine eyes shall behold, and not another;
         my reins are consumed with hope within me.
28.   If you shall say, "Why did we persecute him?"
         the root of the matter is found in me.
29.   Be ye afraid of the sword:
         for wrath bringeth the punishments of the
            sword,
         that ye may know there is a judgment.

Because Bildad in his second discoure (ch. 18) has
just insinuated that Job was to become merely an awful
example for East and West (18:19-21), there is little

[2] Hebrew obscure, text uncertain.

else for the patient to do in his reply than to wish his
friends a sense of shame (19:3). They have refused to
consider that God has fenced him up like a captured
unicorn (vs. 8*a*). The image is apt. Pain singles a man
out of the crowd and separates him even from his most
intimate circle. George Bernard Shaw may well make
Don Juan jest, "Heaven is all right, of course, but for
meeting friends and acquaintances, you can't beat hell."
He knows, underneath the laughter, that hell is precisely solitude in company, "that empty too-much," as
Rilke called it. Job now experiences this kind of estrangement. Society has spewed him out as marked by
the Deity, and tainted. With painstaking fastidiousness,
the hero catalogues one by one the members of his community, beginning with the more distant ones and tight-
ening the knot toward the more intimate ones. The
phrases unroll without pause, and the emotion wells up
as an orchestral crescendo upon a monotone (vss. 13-19).

All have repudiated him: his brethren in the larger
sense of the term, fellow tribesmen; his acquaintances,
with whom he exchanged casual pleasantries; his kin-
folk who belonged to his own clan, issued of a common
ancestor whom they had known and revered; his familiar friends, members of his club; the guests of his house
who were indebted to his kindness, impoverished distant
cousins, perhaps, or outlaws of obscure origin whom he
had sheltered and fed for years with no questions asked;
his maidservants who took care of his household; his
own slave, who served him personally; his wife; his full
brothers; even infants and boys and girls who stumbled
on his path and teased him with trusting insolence;
finally, the friends of his secret circle: no doubt, Eliphaz, Bildad and Zophar, who had come from afar at

great inconvenience to themselves, men whom he truly loved. All of these have excommunicated him.

Apprehending the edge of the abyss on which he now stands (the expression, "I am escaped with the skin of my teeth" is susceptible of a score of translations and interpretations; it probably means, "I am between life and death"), his anger wanes and his social pride at last weakens. He so yearns for communion and understanding that he will beg for pity. He even will beg twice.

> Have pity upon me, have pity upon me, O ye my
> friends! (Vs. 21a.)

Exactly the same prayer as that of the psalmist to God, *"Kyrie eleison, Miserere mei,"* which in Old English was rendered with a directly transitive verb, "Grace me" (Ps. 51:1). This is the prayer of surrender, but Job has not directed it to God. This is the supplication which appeals to the passion of mercy, to the longing of a mother for the fruit of her womb. But Job cannot offer this prayer to the Deity:

> For it is the hand of God which hath struck me (vs. 21b).

Solitude is not only the result of suffering that isolates a stricken individual from a community at ease, healthy, and dull. It *is* suffering itself. As physical pain and mental grief make any entourage suspicious, thereby creating loneliness—the pith of sorrow—it in turn leads the sufferer to concentrate on his egocentricity and develops in him an attitude of defiance, bitterness and hatred for the community.

Tennessee Williams wrote in his preface to *The Rose*

Tatoo, "Men pity and love each other more deeply than they permit themselves to know," but he paid homage to grace in man rather than to human nature. Elsewhere, as in his preface to *Cat on a Hot Tin Roof,* he more realistically spoke of "a lonely condition, so terrifying to think of that we usually don't," and concluded, "Personal lyricism is the outcry of prisoner to prisoner from the cell in solitary where each is confined for the duration of his life."

The thought of a relation between literary or artistic creation and solitude may well have been in the mind of the Joban poet, for it was immediately after the denial of and response to his appeal of solitariness that Job uttered the wish,

Oh that my words were now written! (Vs. 23*a*.)

Want of comprehension today may induce one to settle for literary fame tomorrow. But how soon will men be able to understand? Let some kind of permanence be assured:

Oh that they were engraved on a scroll of brass!
(Vs. 23*b*.)

Parchment or papyrus are too ephemeral; where is a roll of metal leaves, or better, a rocky wall where a stylus of iron and lead alloy will engrave my poem forever? The allusion may be to a certain cliff in Lebanon, near the Nahr el-Kelb, where military conquerors from the dawn of imperial history down to Bonaparte and Allenby have recorded the exploits of their armies.

Job soon discerns the futility of literary fame. What

does it matter to him, *hic et nunc,* if twenty-five centuries
hence, strange critics and readers peer over his verse?
Moreover, as Melville wrote to Hawthorne in 1851:

All Fame is patronage. Let me be infamous. . . .
Think of it! To go down to posterity is bad enough,
any way; but to go down as a "man who lived among the
cannibals!" When I speak of posterity, in reference to
myself, I only mean the babies who will probably be
born in the moment immediately ensuing upon my giving up the ghost. . . . I have come to regard this matter
of Fame as the most transparent of all vanities.

Indeed, like all men too courageous or visionary for
their times, Job lived among cannibals.

> Why do ye persecute me as God,
>   and are not sated with my flesh? (Vs. 22.)

Here is the dead end of solitude. The hero turns around
the impasse and finds an exit only through an acrobatic
and unexpected twist. "But as for me, I know . . ."
(vs. 25*a*).
   Is the leap of faith a betrayal of weariness? Many
would think so.

> It is utter
> Terror and loneliness
> That drive a man to address the Void as "Thou."

To this bit of "Conversation at Midnight," by Edna St.
Vincent Millay, Graham Greene echoes in *The End of
the Affair,* "We have to delude ourselves into a belief
in God. . . ." Or in *The Quiet American,* "Wouldn't we

all do better not trying to understand, accepting the
fact that no human being will ever understand another,
not a wife a husband, a lover a mistress, nor a parent a
child? Perhaps that's why men have invented God—a
being capable of understanding. Perhaps if I wanted
to be understood or to understand, . . . I would bam-
boozle myself into belief."

Is Job going to capitulate, creating a God whom he
desperately needs? In his essay on Job, *God's Lonely
Man,* Thomas Wolfe confides, "To live alone . . . a
man should have the confidence of God, the tranquil
faith of a monastic saint, the stern impregnability of
Gibraltar." Is not Job's imminent leap of faith a search
for the false consolations of religion, precisely a devious
equivalent of what the friends wish him to do: to repent
and obtain security? Will Job yield to the supreme
temptation, accept a technique by which he might escape
the contradictions of existence? The answer depends
upon the nature and function of the redeemer whose
life he now proclaims:

But as for me, I know that my redeemer liveth,
  . . . and from within my flesh I shall see God
  (19:25-26).

There are few passages in the poem or in the entire
Bible which are as well known as this one. Its interpretation, however, and even its original text are highly uncertain. As it is true practically for all scriptural
passages which have been used in theological polemics,
either among later Jewish factions or between Judaism
and Christianity, the Hebrew manuscripts and the
ancient versions offer such a bewildering diversity of

readings that any translation will remain largely conjectural.[3]

The first and last lines of the paragraph are relatively
clear (vss. *25a* and *26b*) but the text of the intermediary
clauses (vss. *25b* and *26a*) is seriously corrupt. In the
Old Testament in general, the person of a "redeemer"
is more than the "avenger of the blood" (II Sam.
14:11). He may be the next of kin whose duty is to raise
a posterity to the dead man or whose privilege is a first
option at the dead man's estate (Deut. 25:5-10; Ruth
2:20; 3:9; 4:4 ff.; cf. Lev. 25:25; Num. 5:8). In extended use, the word may be applied to the defender of
the oppressed, especially God, the "redeemer" of Israel
(Exod. 6:6; Isa. 41:14; etc.) and individuals (Ps.
69:18; etc.) whom he delivers from persecution, evil
and death. Consequently, many exegetes understand the
phrase "My redeemer is alive" and as referring to God
himself. According to this view, Job will die, but at the
edge of his grave ("upon the dust," vs. *25b*) the eter-
nally Living One will stand and appear to Job in a
vision. Although "without" his flesh, Job will see God.

Other commentators correctly translate "within my
flesh" but maintain that the poet here anticipates the
"vision" of the Lord from the whirlwind (chs. 38 ff.).
The latter part of this statement is not likely to be ac-
ceptable. Whatever Job may have said in verses *25b* and
26a (and the translation proposed above is little more
than hypothetical—not demonstrated beyond challenge), he expected to die. The mention of the "dust"
(vs. *25b*) implies certainly the idea of death and burial

[3] For a summary of the textual and exegetical problems, see Terrien,
"Introduction and Exegesis of the Book of Job," *The Interpreter's Bible,*
Vol. III, pp. 1051 ff.

(cf. 7:21; 10:9; 17:16; 20:11; 34:15; Ps. 104:29; etc.). At the same time, the point of vision is described as "from within my flesh," stressing concrete vitality and the identity of personal existence, after death, with individual consciousness as it is experienced now. Moreover, Job can hardly speak of God as "his redeemer," since in the same breath he adds that through the agency of the latter he will see God. The figure of the redeemer appears to belong to the same motif as that of the mediator (9:33), the heavenly witness and advocate (16:19) who will "maintain the right of a man with God" (16:21).

The hero's expectation seems to be precisely that God is not his redeemer! In fact, the Lord never "appeared" to Job "from the whirlwind" (ch. 38), but he spoke—a distinction which in Hebrew theology is of extreme importance. Man on earth never sees God (not even Moses who attempted to force the Deity into sensorial manifestation, Exod. 33:13-23).

A fragment from the proto-Phoenician liturgy of a season festival may suggest a background for the poet's imagery. The worshiper who in the ancient town of Ugarit (Ras Shamra) celebrated the ritual of the dying and rising God repeated the rubric,

> And I know that the strong lord liveth,
> Eternal is the prince, lord of the earth.

Perhaps unconsciously transposing the mythopoetic language of his cultural environment and adapting it to Hebraic monotheism, the poet was attempting to describe, without the help of any approved terminology, a new spiritual insight.

Job's social isolation is as complete as his estrangement from God. No next of kin will ever rise after his death to avenge his blood or to vindicate his honor. Not even the generations of a future humanity, with their "verdict of history," can satisfy his craving. But he has a redeemer. He knows that. This redeemer, however, will accomplish both less and more than the term usually suggests he might do. Less, because Job at this moment gives up the idea of vindication. More, because the redeemer will bring him, after death, into the very presence of God Almighty.

To see God! This is now his only desire. He does not say that he will be avenged. He does not pretend that he will live forever. He does not claim that God will recognize his integrity. He is totally reticent on the "benefits" or "enjoyment" which may be derived from the prospective meeting. But he does say that the presence of God will be real, complete and sufficient. He insists on the quality of his post-mortem identity with his present self and he tells of his impatience:

I, even I, not another. I shall see him,
  and mine own eyes shall see, not a stranger!
  My reins are consumed with hope within me (vs. 27).

The emphasis, by repetition and choice of vocabulary, is obvious. It appears to indicate that Job tries to anticipate contradiction. Most likely, his friends are giving signs, either by gesture, word or attitude, of their opposition. Besides, Job may fear that, even if he sees God beyond the grave, he may not truly be identical with his present personality. A shade or a ghost is not endowed with the full consciousness of existence. But he insists: "from within my flesh, as a concrete, vital, substantial, responsible, fully characterized person, I shall see God. Not as a disincarnate, disembodied entity, but I, even I, my total self."

If the above interpretation is correct, Job is breaking the age-long Hebraic reluctance to accept life eternal, but he is not yet stating the later concept of the resurrection of the flesh as a gift of rebirth by the God who creates life (cf. the little apocalypse now incorporated in Isaiah, especially 26:19, and the visions of Daniel, 12:2 ff.). He merely knows that death will not be the end and that he will be brought at last before the very face of the Divine.

The word "redeemer" is still well-chosen, for in this sense, Job will be delivered from that which torments him most sharply, the absence of God.

Still be with me, who then at the summit of human
    endeavour
And scaling the highest, man's thought could, gazed
    hopeless as ever
On the new stretch of Heaven above me—till, mighty
    to save,
Just one lift of thy hand cleared that distance—God's
    throne from man's grave!

The words of Robert Browning in "Saul" are modern and they do not offer an adequate commentary of Job's new faith. Nevertheless, they stress the loss of man's initiality. Job's certitude does not represent a cheapening of his faith but it implies a momentary eclipse of his pride. Job's certitude does not suggest that he has fallen for what Karl Barth calls "a mist or concoction of religion." Job's certitude is held at the same cost as ever. It is not an illusion of emotionalism induced by grief and the fear of the void. It is absolute faith because it is complete waiting—albeit impatient—upon the good pleasure of divine availability.

If the experience of religion is more than a void, or claims to contain or to possess or to "enjoy" God, it is a shameless and abortive anticipation of that which can proceed from the unknown God alone.[4]

Thus the summit of Job's reach in his struggle does not attenuate his despair in the present conditions of his existence. And the third cycle of discussion will find him at a level of despondency as low as before, and in some respects lower than ever before. In spite of the tortures which are still inflicted upon him, he does not seek refuge in the benevolence of a friendly God. He respects completely the mystery of holiness, with its beyondness and its dread. But he shows man's need for a Christ.

Inasmuch as the replies of Job to the third discourses of the friends have been preserved, not in a complete form but in an editorially truncated way, one may speculate and ask whether the declaration on the redeemer and the vision of God (19:25 ff.) constituted originally the climax of Job's search. At any rate, the crimson thread shows clearly its stitches through the heavy tapestry: a God-man, a mediator, a witness and advocate, a redeemer. The terminology may be awkward and the thought obscure, but the consistency of the spiritual growth is evident. Man moves slowly but steadily from the wish to assert his autonomy to the impatience of merely facing the fullness of God Almighty.

Christian faith is not to be sought in the poem of Job, but in it as in the Psalms and in the poems of the Prophets, one may see much more than a record of estrange-

[4] Karl Barth, *The Epistle to the Romans* (London: Oxford University Press, 1938), p. 50.

ment. One discerns a force which begets, within Hebraic
monotheism, the faith in God through a Christ. While
the historical emergence of New Testament Christology
depends upon the influence of many diverse factors—
such as Messianic hope, high-priestly ritual and Temple
cultic presence, hypostatic concepts of Word, Wisdom,
Spirit and Law, together with the Hellenistic impact
of the mystery worship of a dying and rising god—a
genuinely Hebraic need for reconciliation with a transcending Deity provided the catalytic element. This
need appears in many places in the Old Testament but
nowhere more clearly than in the poem of Job. In this
sense, Christians are able to sing Händel's famous
aria, "I know that my Redeemer liveth," in the context
of the gospel. Job is *God's Lonely Man,* who might
have said, "I go before my thoughts into exile, at the
head of a great procession of silence."[5] "His solitude is
a prophet's solitude," like that of Jeremiah, a prede-
cessor of the Joban poet, or that of Second Isaiah, a
successor, who painted the suffering servant of the Lord
as "a man of sorrow." For such men, *"La solitude dé-
gage un certain degré d'égarement sublime. C'est la
fumée du buisson ardent"* (Victor Hugo). "Solitude
releases a certain degree of sublime aberration, like the
smoke of the burning bush." Job knows that he will see
God. He does not know whether or not he will be saved.
A God who would promise to save him might be an
idol. "God is not an explanation of the world's enigmas
or a guarantee for our salvation. He is an eternal challenge, an urgent demand. He is not a problem to be
solved but a question addressed to us as individuals, as
nations, as mankind."[6]

---

[5] Léon Bloy, in Albert Béguin, *A Study in Impatience,* p. 4.
[6] Abraham Heschel, *Man Is Not Alone,* p. 92.

Chapter 6

The Ignorance and Arrogance of Religion

ZOPHAR has not discerned in Job's groping agony any inkling of the true issue (ch. 20). He has not seen that Job is after the gratuitous love of God for man and the gratuitous love of man for God. The closed mind of static nonthinking stimulates Job to explore further and further the scandal of human life as he knows it, not only in his own flesh but also among men in general.

I

The Anomaly of Happiness

Job's Reply to the Second Discourse of Zophar, 21:1-34

i

21:2.   Hear diligently my speech:
         grant me at least this consolation.
   3.   Suffer me that I may speak;
         and after that I have spoken, mock on.
   4.   As for me, is my complaint against man?
         Is it without cause that my spirit is impatient?

5. Look at me and be astonished,
　　and lay your hand upon your mouth.
6. Even I, when I think of it, I am afraid,
　　and shuddering taketh hold of my flesh.

ii

7. Wherefore do the wicked live,
　　become old, yea, are mighty in power?
8. Their seed is established in their sight with them,
　　and their offspring before their eyes.
9. Their houses are safe from fear,
　　neither is the rod of God upon them.
10. Their bull gendereth, and faileth not;
　　their cow calveth, and casteth not her calf.
11. They send forth their little ones like a flock,
　　and their children dance.
12. They sing with the timbrel and harp,
　　and rejoice at the sound of the pipe.
13. They spend their days in wealth,
　　and in peace go down to the grave.

iii

14. Nevertheless, they say unto God, Depart from
　　us;
　　for we desire not the knowledge of thy ways.
15. What is the Almighty, that we should serve
　　him?
　　and what profit should we have, if we pray
　　unto him?
16. Behold, is not their happiness in their hand?
　　The designs of the wicked are far from God.[1]
17. How oft is the candle of the wicked put out!
　　and how oft cometh their destruction upon
　　them!
　　how oft doth God distribute sorrows in his
　　anger?

---

[1] With the LXX.

18.   How oft are they as stubble before the wind,
          and as chaff that the storm carrieth away?

iv

19.   [You say:] God layeth up his iniquity for his
          children!
          [No!] Let God punish him, that he may
          know!
20.   Let his eyes see his own destruction,
          and let him drink of the wrath of the Al-
          mighty!
21.   For what doth he care for his house after him,
          when the number of his months is cut off?
22.   But shall any teach God knowledge,
          seeing he judgeth from on high?

v

23.   One dieth in his full strength,
          being wholly at ease and quiet.
24.   His breasts are full of fat,
          and his bones are moistened with marrow.
25.   And another dieth in the bitterness of his soul,
          and never tasteth happiness.
26.   They shall lie down alike in the dust,
          and the worms shall cover them.
27.   Behold, I know your thoughts,
          and the devices you imagine to wrong me.
28.   For ye say, Where is the house of the tyrant?
          and where are the dwelling places of the
          wicked?

vi

29.   Have ye not asked them that go by the way?
          and do ye not know the tales they tell?
30.   That the wicked is spared in the day of calamity,
          that he is exempt on the day of wrath?
31.   Who shall reproach his behavior to his face?
          and who shall repay him for what he hath
          done?

32. When he shall be carried in pomp to the grave,
      a watch shall be kept upon his tomb.
33. The clods of the valley shall be sweet unto him;
      every man shall follow his funeral,
            and before him, a procession without number.
34. How then comfort ye me in vain,
      seeing in your answers there remaineth false-
            hood?

Driving in the rut, Zophar in his second discourse
(ch. 20) likened Job to the hypocrite and the godless,
whose outward show of piety and moral behavior does
not correspond to inward intent. The joy of such a man,
said he, is but for a moment (20:5); "he will perish
for ever like his own dung" (20:7a). Job replies (ch.
21) by pointing out the anomaly of happiness. The
theme of the prosperity of the wicked is dear to the Old
Testament in general and to the psalmists in particular,
most of whom were dispossessed Levites, the landless
singers of the cultic pageantry which surrounded Temple worship, at least after the Reform of Josiah (621
B.C.). Job, as a rich man now destitute, remarks that
history disproves the dogma of poetic justice. Happiness does not follow "the rules of the game." It is an
anomalous occurrence. Some have it "in their hand"
(vs. 16). They do not even need to pray for it (vs. 15).
They do not even share in the common error of the
"profitability of religion." They say,

What is the Almighty, that we should serve him?
    and what profit should we have, if we pray unto
      him? (Vs. 15.)

They do not even "serve God for nought" (1:9) since
they do not need to serve God at all! Yet their brash

arrogance meets with total impunity. Death hits all men indiscriminately (21:23-25). The wicked man, however, seems to be more often spared than the righteous (vss. 30-31), and after a magnificent funeral,

> The clods of the valley are sweet to him (vs. 33*a*),

an expression common to the folk sayings of mankind, echoed in the Latin phrase, *Sic tibi terra levis*.

There is, however, one aspect of the human situation which is more scandalous than the anomaly of happiness: it is the anomaly of misery, when God is absent from those who need him.

II

The Absence of God

Job's Reply to the Third Discourse of Eliphaz,
23:1—24:17, 25

i

23:2. Even today is my complaint rebellious:
      The hand of God[1] is heavier than my groaning.

  3. Oh that I knew where I might find him!
      that I might come even to his seat!

  4. I would lay my case before him,
      and fill my mouth with arguments.

[1] With the LXX and Syriac.

5.   I would learn the words which he would answer
me,
    and understand what he would say unto me.
6.   Would he plead against me with his great power?
    No! He would have only to pay heed to me.
7.   There the righteous might dispute with him;
    and I should win for ever a judgment of ac-
quittal.[2]

ii

8.   Behold, I go eastward, but he is not there;
    and westward, but I cannot perceive him:
9.   Northward, where he doth work, but I cannot
behold him:
    I turn[3] southward, but I cannot see him.
10.   Yet he knoweth the way that I take:
    Let him try me: I shall come forth as gold.
11.   My foot hath held his steps;
    his ways have I kept, and have not turned
aside.
12.   Neither have I gone back from the command-
ment of his lips;
    I have treasured in my bosom[4] the words of
his mouth.

iii

13.   But he is in one mind, and who can turn him?
    and what his soul desireth even that he doeth.
14.   For he performeth the thing that is appointed
for me:
    and many such things are with him.
15.   Therefore am I terrified at his presence:
    when I consider, I am in dread of him.
16.   For God hath shattered my heart,
    and the Almighty hath affrighted me.

[2] With the LXX.
[3] With Syriac and Vulgate.
[4] With the LXX and Vulgate.

17.   I am cut off, but not on account of darkness,
          nor is it the shadow that covereth my face.

iv

24:1.   Why, seeing times are not hidden from the
             Almighty,
          do they that know him not see his days?
2.   Some remove the landmarks;
          they violently take away flocks and feed
             thereof.
3.   They drive away the ass of the fatherless,
          they take the widow's ox for a pledge.
4.   They turn the needy out of the way,
          the poor of the earth hide themselves together.
5.   Behold, as wild asses in the desert,
          go they forth to their work;
       Rising before dawn for a prey,
          seeking in the wilderness food for their
             young.
6.   They reap every one his corn in the field,
          and they glean what remaineth in the vineyard
             of the rich.[5]

v

7.   They lie naked, lodging without clothing,
          and have no covering in the cold.
8.   They are wet with the showers of the mountains,
          and embrace the rock for want of a shelter.
9.   The fatherless is plucked from the breast,
          and the infant of the poor taken in pledge.
10.   They go about naked without clothing,
          hungry, they carry the sheaves,
11.   And press oil in the olive groves;
          thirsty, they tread the wine presses.

[5] Hebrew obscure.

12. From the city rise the groans of the dying,
        and the soul of the wounded crieth for help:
     yet God payeth no heed to their prayer.[6]

vi

13. There are also those that rebel against the light:
        they know not the ways thereof,
        nor abide in the paths thereof.
14. The murderer rising in the dark,
        killeth the poor and needy,
        and the thief roameth[7] in the night.
15. The eye also of the adulterer waiteth for the twi-
        light,
        saying, No eye shall see me! and disguiseth his
        face.
16. In the dark robbers dig through houses,
        which they have marked for themselves in
        daytime;
        they know not the light.
17. For all of them, the morning is as the deep
        shadow;
        for they are friends with the terrors of the
        shadow of death.[8]
25. If it be not so, now, who will make me a liar,
        and declare my speech worthless?

On earlier occasions, the quest for the self-disclosure
of God led the hero to formulate his desire for a mediator, a heavenly witness and a redeemer. The same desire
is made more urgent than ever by the disquisitions of

[6] Vocalizing with the Syriac the Hebrew consonantal text to read *tephillāh*,
"prayer," instead of *tiphlāh*, "folly."

[7] Hebrew obscure. Probably read *yehallekh gannābh* instead of *yehi
kaggannābh*.

[8] Omitting verses 18-24 which probably belonged originally to the third
discourse of Zophar, now editorially placed in the mouth of Job.

Eliphaz on divine impassiveness (22:2-3). Job resumes his search with renewed passion:

Oh that I knew where I might find him! (23:3a.)

The attempt is futile, for God does not belong to the realm of created space:

Behold, I go eastward, but he is not there (vs. 8a).

Although the poet was influenced by a mythological motif from an ancient Semitic cosmogony in his reference to the north "where God works" (vs. 9a), he shows that no confusion may be made between the Creator and the created universe.

The theme of the absence of God haunts the whole Bible, from the dereliction of early Israel, "when there were no prophets," to the sense of desolation in the psalmists, especially the poet of Psalm 22 whom Jesus quoted upon the cross (cf. Mark 15:34; Matt. 27:46). The Scripture is too easily called the record of revelation. Moses and the Prophets, like Jesus and the early Christians—not excluding contemporary ones—faced the empty dread of the unknown, where there is no vision, no spirit, no courage, no purpose, no voice, no presence.

Verily, thou art a God that hidest thyself! (Isa. 45:15.)

This is the exclamation of Israel throughout the ages as well as of the Church, and the biblical insistence on the

"word of God" is only matched by the biblical acquaintance with the *Deus absconditus* who, as if in disgust
from the human experiment, would

"Adjourn . . ."
"To that farther side of skies."[9]

Secularists sometimes envy the so-called men of faith,
thinking that professed religionists, at least, find a solace
in the presence of God in time of danger or loneliness,
but mystics and saints know as well as Job that God es-
capes their search. And they must resist the temptation
of accepting easy comfort through an illusory company
with the creation of their despair, precisely because they
trust only a God who is truly God. Job, by bewailing
the absence of the maker of the worlds, once again reveals his theological integrity. He cannot make a God
in his image, a God who should love him. He is in utter
dread of the desert but he cannot people that desert with
a figment of his desire.

There is a rigor and a truth in the story of the Bedouin
guide who led a traveler over a mountain pass after a
night spent at the oasis in the valley which was now far
below them. As he stopped his mount at the top of the
track, he contemplated for a long moment the new vista
of sand wastes which had just opened ahead of them.
Inhaling deeply the pure, dry, clean, empty and odor-
less wind of the desert, he said, "Can you still smell the
exquisite fragrance of the orchards behind us? Its head-
iness is that of wine and its warmth a woman's. But do
you now smell the wind of the wilderness? It is the

---

[9] Peter Viereck, "Incantation at Assisi."

breath of God." For Job, God the Void appears again like God the Enemy (vss. 13-17).

He hath shattered my intellect and will (vs. 16*a*).

Rising to the perspective of humanity at bay on a world-wide scope, Job now acquires a new stature. No longer lamenting on account of a self-centered concern, he borrows the vantage point of the universal poor. Like the prophet Amos and his successors, Job takes up the case for all the oppressed, the hungry and the naked (24:1-6, 7-12), summing up with the cry,

Yet God payeth no attention to their prayer (vs. 12*c*).

On account of Job, the Bible has taken within itself all the attacks which have been made against God by a crucified humanity. No tragic poet has outdone this bit of worldly skepticism. Dostoevsky in *The Brothers Karamazov* describes a scene in which a young child was stripped naked in the cold winter morning and made to run in front of a pack of hunting dogs because he had thrown a stone at one of them. "I understand solidarity in retribution," comments Ivan, "but there can be no solidarity with children. . . . Some jester will say, perhaps, that the child would have grown up and have sinned, but you see he didn't grow up, he was torn to pieces by the dogs, at eight years old. . . . I don't want the mother to embrace the oppressor who threw her son to the dogs! She dare not forgive him! . . . I would rather remain with my unavenged suffering and unsatisfied indignation, *even if I were wrong*."

Indignation for the suffering of others may lead to

revolt more readily than the experience of self-endured grief. Job is indignant and God remains absent.

> And one feels slipping into the dark spiral
> Of abyss where Job, Thales, Epicurus have fall'n,
> Where one goes agroping for someone in the pit,
> When man says, Answer! and God is not able.

A Romantic poet like Victor Hugo will give up belief in omnipotence in order to safeguard a loving Deity, but he does not see that a God who strives is no longer a God, or that love at the theological level as well as in the psychological realm must have power or not be.

Others, shuddering before the same horrors, have been led to worship. "Everything that happens to me," wrote Léon Bloy, "calls for adoration. . . . Man has places in his heart which do not yet exist, and into them enters suffering, in order to bring them into existence." And thus Helen Waddell portrays *Peter Abelard* facing the reality, most aggressive in its negativity, of the *Deus absconditus*:

> He saw no heavens opened: he saw no Son of Man. For a moment it seemed to him that all the vital forces in his body were withdrawing themselves, that the sight had left his eyes and the blood was ebbing from his heart: he felt the grey breath of dissolution, the falling asunder of body and soul. For a moment: then his spirit leapt toward heaven in naked adoration. Stripped of all human emotion, with no warmth of contrition, with no passion of devotion, but with every power of his mind, with every pulse of his body, he worshipped God.

The mind of Job was not ripe for this leaping up of

spirit, for the morality of his religion remained a formidable obstacle to his adoration.

III

The Tragedy of Integrity

Job's Reply to the Third Discourse of Bildad,
26:1-4; 27:1-12

i

26:2. How hast thou helped him, that is without
           power?
        [God!] how savest thou the arm that hath no
           strength?
3. How hast thou counseled him that hath no
           wisdom?
        and how hast thou to the ignorant[1] declared
           the thing as it is?
4. To whom hast thou uttered words?
        and whose spirit came from thee?

ii

27:2. As God liveth, who hath taken away my right;
        and the Almighty, who hath vexed my soul:
3. As long as my life is in me,
        and the breath of God is in my nostrils,
4. My lips shall not speak falsehood,
        nor my tongue utter deceit.
5. God forbid that I should say you are right:
        till I die I will not remove mine integrity from
        me.
6. My righteousness I hold fast, and will not let
        it go:

[1] Reading with one Hebrew MS *labbur* instead of *larobh*.

my heart shall not reproach me so long as I
live.

iii

7. Let mine enemy be as the wicked,
    and he that riseth up against me as the un-
      righteous.
8. For what is the hope of the hypocrite, though he
      hath gained,
    when God taketh away his soul?
9. Will God hear his cry,
    when trouble cometh upon him?
10. Will he delight himself in the Almighty?
    will he always call upon God?
11. I will illumine you on the hand of God,
    that which is with the Almighty will I not
      conceal.
12. Behold, all ye yourselves have seen it;
    why then are ye thus altogether vain?

The significance of this truncated fragment of Job's
reply to the third discourse of Bildad (25:1-6; 26:5-14,
as hypothetically reconstituted), lies in the fact that it
begins with another defiant prayer of Job. Couched in
the second person singular, the first strophe (26:2-4) is
not to be considered as addressed to Bildad, for Job is
not in the habit of singling out his interlocutors. Here
is a prayer of defiance which is not tamed by the tinge of
tenderness. No love-dialogue motif is to be found in its
cool questioning. It is indeed a thrust at divine hiddenness, secretiveness, remoteness, inactivity. According to
the theology of Hebraism and popular religion in all
ages everywhere, God helps and saves in the realm of
history, God makes himself known and his will clear by
the commandments of his law, God discloses his ulti-

mate purpose through the ministry of his prophets. Job asks three sets of double questions, covering precisely the three chief areas of official religion, and he finds that the Deity has failed the test. God is no helper or savior (26:2), no counselor or teacher (vs. 3), no giver of the word or inspirer (vs. 4). Nothing more is left for Job to do than to declare under oath ("As God liveth!" 27:2) that he shall never recant. The drama is that of his virtue. The tragedy, that of his integrity (vs. 5*b*). Men cling to the idea they have of themselves with the bourgeois tenacity of bookkeepers. Job is the victim of a religion which succeeds in producing morality.

The words of James Muilenburg, although written about Jeremiah, fit Job almost as well:

> Precisely because he is so intensely religious, so intensely near to God, he is most in need of repenting. His intensely religious mood has actually separated him ... from God.[2]

God is absent because man has not renounced his claim to reach him.

IV

The Inaccessibility of Wisdom

28:1-28

i

28:1. Surely there is a vein for the silver,
        and a place for gold where they fine it.
  2.   Iron is taken out of the earth,
        and brass is molten out of the stony ore.

---

[2] James Muilenburg in the *Union Seminary Quarterly Review*, IV, 2 (Jan. 1949, p. 18.

3. Man setteth an end to darkness,
      and searcheth out to the farthest bound
        the stones of darkness and the deep shadow.
4. He slitteth mine shafts in a valley away from
        human habitation.
      Miners are forgotten, away from the beaten
        path;
      they hang afar from men, swinging to and fro.

5. As for the earth, out of it cometh bread;
      but underneath it is molten as it were fire.
6. The stones of it are the place of sapphires:
      and it hath dust of gold.
7. Its path no bird of prey knoweth,
      and the falcon's eye hath not seen it.
8. The wild beasts have not trodden it,
      nor the fierce lion passed by it.

9. Man putteth forth his hand upon the flinty rock:
      he overturneth the mountains by the roots.
10. He cutteth out river beds among the rocks;
      and his eye seeth every precious thing.
11. He bindeth the streams in time of flood,
      and the thing that is hid bringeth he forth to
        light.

12. *But where shall wisdom be found?*
      and where is the place of understanding?
13. *Man knoweth not the way thereof;*
      neither is it found in the land of the living.

ii

14. The deep saith, It is not in me:
      and the sea saith, It is not with me.
15. It cannot be gotten for gold,
      neither shall silver be weighed for the price
        thereof.

16.   It cannot be valued with the gold of Ophir,
     with the precious onyx, or the sapphire.

17.   The gold and the glass cannot equal it,
     nor can it be exchanged for jewels of fine gold.
18.   No mention shall be made of coral or crystal,
     for the price of wisdom is above pearls.
19.   The topaz of Ethiopia shall not equal it,
     neither shall it be valued with pure gold.

20.   *Whence then cometh wisdom?*
     and where is the place of understanding?
21.   *Seeing it is hid from the eyes of all living,*
     and kept close from the fowls of the air.

iii

22.   Destruction and death say,
     We have heard the fame thereof with our ears.
23.   God understandeth the way thereof,
     and he knoweth the place thereof.
24.   For he looketh to the ends of the earth,
     and seeth under the whole heaven.

25.   When he gave to the wind its weight;
     and meted out the waters by measure;
26.   When he made a decree for the rain;
     and a way for the lightning of the thunder;
27.   Then did he see it, and declare it;
     he prepared it, yea, and searched it out.

28.   And unto man he said,
     Behold, the fear of the Lord, this is wisdom,
     And to depart from evil is understanding.

It is difficult to suppose that Job uttered these magnificent lines at this stage of his spiritual parturition,
between the debate proper (chs. 3-27) and the peroration (chs. 29-31). Because the hymn on the inaccessibil-

ity of wisdom concludes with the gnomic motto of Orthodox Judaism (28:28), most interpreters believe that
it did not belong to the original poem of Job. They
cogently argue that Job could not have contradicted so
completely and so abruptly his preceding attacks on an
impassive Deity (ch. 26) or his succeeding challenge
to the morality of God (chs. 29-31). On the other hand,
a careful scrutiny of the text of the hymn as a whole
shows a close affinity with the language and thought of
the discourses of the Lord (chs. 38 ff.), which in turn
quite clearly originate with the poet of the dialogue.
The difficulty arises only in connection with the concluding verse. Inasmuch as its form impairs the paral-
lelism of the preceding refrains (vss. 12 and 20), the
disturbing quality of its moralistic thought loses its impact: in verse 28, wisdom is no longer a divine preroga-
tive inacessible to human beings; it has become a way
of life fully within the reach of moral man. In all probability, verse 28 has been editorially substituted for an
original third refrain parallel to the other two in form
as well as in thought.

The hymn had most likely a function similar to that
of the chorus in a Greek tragedy. While the action mo-
mentarily rested in a sort of open-stage intermission, a
solitary voice or a choir chanted a gradual-like aria as
an artistic and psychological anticipation of the Voice
from the Whirlwind.

The poem presents itself in three strophic groups:
The first group (vss. 1-13) praises the technological
skill of man only to offset this *gloria in excelsis homini*
by the admission: wisdom is not within the reach of
human art or science. Man's conquest of nature should
not fool him. His behavior does not fit his newly ac-
quired powers. The irony of culture, either that of

Babylon in the sixth century B.C. or that of the West
in the twentieth century A.D., lies in the simple fact that
homo faber is always one step ahead of *homo sapiens*!
Through the power of his arm, man can lull himself
into believing that "he has arrived." But as T. S. Eliot
reminds him, in *East Coker,*

> The serenity only a deliberate hebetude,
> The wisdom only the knowledge of dead secrets
> Useless in the darkness into which they peered
> Or from which they turned their eyes.

The second group (vss. 14-22) attacks the cultic rituals
which attempt to conciliate the forces of chaos (vs. 14)
and the underworld (vs. 22) to man's ultimate concern:
can he buy life eternal for himself? Wisdom is not to be
found in the mysteries of Egypt or of Mesopotamia,
where men pay huge amounts of wealth in order to secure their *requiem sempiternam.* Red gold, green gold
of Ophir, onyx, sapphire, light pale gold, crystal, coral,
pearls, Ethiopian topaz, even the purest, twice-refined
gold: the wealth of the world will not buy the wisdom
which lasts beyond the ashes. The deep has not received her in her bosom ("she is not in me") nor the
sea as a love mate ("she is not with me"). The divinities
of the lowest hell and the last terror, Abaddon and Mot,
give tantalizing answers, but they have only heard a
whisper of her fame (vs. 22). Religion at shrines and in
cemeteries is futile. Wisdom belongs to God alone. It
is a divine virtue. Nay, a divine child: God saw her,
perceived her existence, computed her growth, tested
her intelligence, conferred upon her the gift of steadfastness and explored her ultimate possibilities (vs. 27).
To pass from this to the present refrain is to descend

from heaven upon earth, to leave God with his awesome
mystery and to frequent man with his illusions of neat
choices and clean-cut decisions. Edith Sitwell perceives
the sorry deflation when she intones "The Poet La-
ments." As soon as men

> ... are taught that goodness means a blinding hour,
> .   .   .   .
> And that Evil can be cast like an old rag,
> And Wisdom caught like a hare and held in the
>   golden sack
> Of the heart. .. ,

someone

> ... must bring back sight to the blind.[1]

If the conventional ending is ignored, the hymnic
interlude receives its full significance. Both the hero
and the friends are gently warned of their limitations,
but Job swiftly transforms his ignorance into arrogance
as he gathers strength for his peroration.

V

The Religious Claims of Morality

Job's Summation to God, 29:1—31:40

Poem 1

The Days of Yesteryear, 29:1-25

i

29:2. Oh that I were as in months past,
            as in the days when God watched over me.

[1] From *The Song of the Cold.*

3. When his candle shined upon my head,
   and when by his light I walked through darkness:
4. As I was in the days of my youth,
   when with a fence God protected my tent;
5. When the Almighty was yet with me,
   when my children were about me;
6. When I washed my steps with butter,
   and the rock poured me out rivers of oil. ....

ii

7. When I went out to the gate through the city,
   when I prepared my seat in the street,
8. The young men saw me, and hid themselves;
   the aged rose, and stood up.
9. The princes refrained from talking,
   and laid their hand on their mouth.
10. The nobles held their peace,
    and their tongue cleaved to the roof of their
    mouth.
11. When the ear heard me, then it blessed me;
    and when the eye saw me, it gave assent to me.

iii

12. Because I delivered the poor that cried,
    and the fatherless, that had none to help him,
13. The blessing of him that was ready to perish
    came upon me:
    and I caused the widow's heart to sing for joy.
14. I put on righteousness, and it clothed me:
    my justice was as a robe and a diadem.
15. I was eyes to the blind,
    and feet was I to the lame.
16. I was a father to the poor:
    and the cause of him I knew not I searched out.

17. And I broke the jaws of the wicked,
     and plucked the spoil out of his teeth.

iv

18. Then I said, I shall die in my nest,
     and I shall multiply my days as the sand.
19. My root was spread out by the waters,
     and the dew lay all night upon my branch.
20. My glory was fresh in me,
     and my bow was renewed in my hand.

v

21. Unto me men gave ear, and waited,
     and kept silence at my counsel.
22. After my words they spake not again;
     and my speech dropped upon them.
23. They waited for me as for the Autumn rain;
     and they opened their mouth wide as for the
     Spring showers.
24. When I smiled at them, they hardly believed it;
     and they watched for the light of my coun-
     tenance.
25. I chose out their way, and sat chief,
     and dwelt as a king in the army,
     as one that comforteth the mourners.

Poem 2

The Trials of the Present, 30:1-31

i

30:1. But now, they have me in derision,
     men that are younger than I,
     whose fathers I would have disdained
     to have set with the dogs of my flock.

2. Yea, whereto might the strength of their hands
        profit me,
      men whose vigor had perished?
3. For want and famine they had wasted away;[1]
      they gnawed the roots of the desolate lands.[1]
4. They picked mallow by the bushes,
      and juniper roots for their meat.
5. They were driven forth from among men,
      people shouted after them as after a thief.
6. They dwelt in the cliffs of the valleys,
      in caves of the earth, and in the rocks.
7. Among the bushes they brayed;
      under the nettles they huddled together.
8. Sons of the fool, yea, a disreputable brood:
      they should have been whipped out of the
        land.

ii

9. And now am I their song,
      yea, I am their byword.
10. They abhor me, they flee far from me,
      and spare not to spit in my face.
11. Because God hath loosed my cord, and afflicted
        me,
      they have also let loose their bridle in my
        presence.
12. Upon my right hand rise their sons;
      they push away my feet;
      and they raise up against me the ways of their
        destruction.

13. They mar my path;
      they set forward my calamity;
      I have no helper.[1]
14. They come upon me as through a wide breach:
      in the desolation they roll in as waves.

[1] Hebrew uncertain.

15. Terrors are turned upon me;
     they pursue my soul as the wind:
     and my welfare passeth away as a cloud.

iii

16. And now my soul is poured out upon me;
     the days of affliction have taken hold of me.
17. My bones are pierced in me in the night season:
     and my sinews[2] take no rest.
18. By great violence my appearance is changed:[2]
     God hath seized me by the collar of my coat,
19. He hath cast me into the mire,
     and I am become like dust and ashes.

20. I cry unto thee, and thou dost not hear me:
     I stand up, and thou regardest me not.[3]
21. Thou art become cruel to me:
     with thy strong hand thou persecutest me.
22. Thou liftest me up to the wind;
     thou causest me to ride upon it,
     and dissolvest my substance.
23. For I know that thou wilt bring me to death,
     and to the house appointed for all living.

iv

24. Whenever someone on a heap of ruins stretched
         out his hand,[2]
     or in distress begged for help,
25. Did I not weep for him that was in trouble?
     was not my soul grieved for the poor?
26. But when I looked for good, then evil came:
     and when I waited for the light,
     then came darkness.

27. My bowels boil and rest not:
     days of affliction come to meet me.

[2] Hebrew uncertain.
[3] With one Hebrew MS and the Vulgate.

28. I go about in mourning without the sun,
    I stand up in the assembly and cry for help.
29. I am a brother to jackals,
    and a companion to ostriches.
30. My sin is black upon me,
    and my bones are burned with heat.
31. My harp also is tuned to dirges,
    and my flute to the weeping of the mourners.

Poem 3

The Oath of Clearance, 31:1-41

i

31:1. I made a covenant with mine eyes;
    why then should I think upon a virgin?
2. Now, what portion of God is there from above?
    and what inheritance of the Almighty from
    on high?
3. Is not destruction to the wicked?
    and disaster to the workers of iniquity?
4. Then, doth not God see my ways,
    and count all my steps?

5. If I have walked with falsehood,
    or if my foot hath hasted to deceit;
6. Let me be weighed in an even balance,
    that God may know mine integrity!
7. If my step hath turned out of the way,
    and mine heart walked after mine eyes,
    and if any blot hath cleaved to mine hands;
8. Then let me sow, and let another eat;
    yea, let my offspring be rooted out!

9. If mine heart have been enticed by a woman,
    or if I have laid wait at my neighbor's door;
10. Then let my wife grind unto another,
    and let others bow down upon her!

11. For this would be a heinous crime;
      yea, an iniquity to be punished by the judge;
12. It would be a fire that consumeth to the lower
      hell,
      and would root out all mine increase.

ii

13. If I did despise the cause of my manservant or of
      my maidservant,
      when they brought a complaint against me;
14. What then shall I do when God riseth up?
      and when he visiteth, what shall I answer?
15. Did not he that made me in the womb make him?
      and did not one God fashion us both alike?

16. If I have withheld the poor from their desire,
      or have caused the eyes of the widow to fail;
17. Or have eaten my morsel myself alone,
      and the fatherless hath not eaten thereof;
18. Whereas from my youth God hath brought me
      up as a father,
      and guided me[4] from my mother's womb;

19. If I have seen any perish for want of clothing,
      or any poor without covering;
20. If his loins have not blessed me,
      and if he were not warmed with the fleece of
      my sheep;
21. If I have lifted up my hand against the father-
      less,
      when I saw protection at the court;

22. Then let mine arm fall from my shoulder blade,
      and mine arm be broken from its socket.

[4] Hebrew uncertain.

23. For the calamity of God was always a dread
        for me:
     I could not stand before his majesty.

iii

24. If I have made gold my hope,
        or have said to the fine gold, Thou art my
        confidence;
25. If I rejoiced because my wealth was great,
        and because mine hand had gotten much;
26. If I beheld the sun when it shined,
        or the moon walking in brightness;
27. And mine heart hath been secretly enticed,
        to blow them a kiss with mine hand:
28. This also were an iniquity to be punished by the
        judge:
     for I should have denied the God that is above.

29. If I rejoiced at the ruin of him that hated me,
        or lifted up myself when evil found him;
30. (Neither have I suffered my mouth to sin
        by wishing a curse to his life.)
31. If the men of my tent had not said,
        Who hath not been sated with meat?
32. (For the stranger did not lodge in the street;
        but I opened my doors to the traveler.)

33. If I covered my transgressions as Adam,
        by hiding mine iniquity in my bosom:
34. If I stood in fear of the multitude,
        and the contempt of the clans terrified me,
        so that I kept silence and went not out of doors;

·   ·   ·   ·   ·   ·   ·   ·   ·   ·   ·   ·

iv

35. Oh that one would hear me!
     Here is my signature! Let the Almighty
        answer me!

> Oh that my opponent had written a book of
> his charges!
36. Surely I would carry it upon my shoulder,
> I would bind it on me as crown.
37. I would give unto him an account of all my steps;
> as a prince would I go near unto him.

38. If my land hath cried out against me,
> or the furrows likewise thereof have wept,
39. If I have eaten the fruits thereof without money,
> or have caused the owners thereof to lose their
> life:
40. Let thistles grow instead of wheat,
> and cockle instead of barley!

(The words of Job are ended.)

Moderns may find Job's summation rather lengthy,
but the three poems have to be read in sequence for they
form a whole to show the culmination of morality both
in its beauty and in its sterility, whenever it assumes the
religious pretense of forcing infinity.

In the first poem (ch. 29), Job dwells upon his past
happiness, which the poet uses as a foil against the present sorrow. In his "post-paradisial afternoon," the hero
remembers his life, now lost, not so much on account of
its material ease (yet, see 29:6) as on account of its op-
portunity for social loving-kindness. Even when he
reminisces about "the Garden of Bliss," he is too discreet in his love for his sons and daughters to speak of
them at length (vs. 5). He dwells, however, on the
public responsibility he assumed in the civic affairs of
his community (vss. 7-11), and more especially on the
generosity with which he succored and defended the

poor (vss. 12-17). He is quite guileless and naïve in
the exposé of his egocentricity. Perhaps he is more
honest and also more virtuous than most of us "who have
a lot to be humble for"! Says e. e. cummings in his
nonlecture 1:

Half a century of time and several continents of space
. . . haven't yet enabled me to locate a single periph-
erally situated ego. . . . My slight acquaintance
with senators pickpockets and scientists leads me to con-
clude that they are far from unselfcentered. So, I believe, are all honest educators. And so (I'm convinced)
are streetcleaners deafmutes murderers mothers, moun-
tainclimbers cannibals fairies, strong men beautiful
women unborn babes international spies, ghostwriters
bums business executives, out and out nuts cranks dope-
fiends policemen, altruists (above all) ambulancechas-
ers obstetricians and liontamers. Not forgetting mor-
ticians. . . .

Like e. e. cummings, the Joban poet knows the peculiar
brand of evil which spoils the supposedly selfless endeavor.

The hero's hope to die at home in a ripe old age (vs.
18) was until recently strengthened by a youthful enjoyment of energy. Incidentally, Jewish and Christian
tradition, no doubt confirmed in the popular mind by
William Blake's engravings, has created the impression
that Job was an old man at the time of his trial. Nothing is further from the truth. Even in the folk tale, his
sons and daughters were still unmarried, a fact which
in the Ancient Near East would suggest that he was an
adult in early maturity, fully possessing his physical and
intellectual vigor. In the poetic discussion, he refers to

himself preferably as a *gébher,* "a strong man,"[5] and notes that even the aged stood up in his presence (29:8*b*), a remark which would be pointless if he were their contemporary. Likewise, Eliphaz and his friends appear to be older than Job's own father (15:10). If Job is a fairly young adult, with children who before their death were in their adolescence, he is acutely aware of his physical weakening. Even more than the actual pain of disease, the loss of his virility probably produces a psychological upheaval which now leads him to speak poetically of his past exploits:

> My root was spread out by the waters,
>   and the dew lay all night upon my branch.
> My glory was fresh in me,
>   and my bow was renewed in my hand
>   (vss. 19-20).

In brief, Job's situation is the more disastrous because he had previously been endowed with the most exceptional gifts. He looked like and had the physical endurance of a Greek god, we might say. He was also successful in the business of living. He was an all-around personality.

The second poem (ch. 30) introduces a dramatic antithesis. "But now" (vs. 1), Job has become a song and a byword to the sons of the beggars he used to feed (vs. 9). God "hath loosed the cord" of his tent (vs. 11) and his existence hangs by a thread at the mercy of the

---

[5] From a verb meaning, "to overflow with strength," and cognate of the noun *gibbôr,* "hero," "champion" (cf. the name of the heavenly agent of divine omnipotence, Gabriel, in later Jewish and Christian angelology). Job often uses the word *gébher* in marked contrast to the word *'ādhām,* "clayman," or *'enôsh,* "mortal man," or even *'îsh,* "husband," "leader." The word *gébher* (like its Aramaic equivalent, *gebhar*) lost in later Hebrew its distinctive meaning of exuberant male, but appears to have preserved it in every Joban context.

storms. But he has enough energy left to attack God once again (vss. 20-23). "Thou art become cruel to me" (vs. 21*a*). In the end, his torture is made of a vast complex, not only physical and social humiliation but also and especially divine estrangement.

The erstwhile strong man is now expecting death, hence his judge, to whom he will shout: "Not Guilty!" Preparing for the day, he repeats the same oath seventeen times.

As has often been remarked, Job's oath of clearance reflects a standard of behavior which is unexcelled either in the Old Testament, the literature of the Ancient Near East and classical Greece, or in the New Testament, not excluding the Sermon on the Mount. The hero not only knows the subtle link which unites the perpetration of a socially harmful act with the psychological mood of the would-be perpetrator, but he also reveals a refinement of social thoughtfulness and generosity which is quite unique in the history of ethics. Moreover, Job justifies his social concern on the basis of brotherhood, which in turn results directly from the fact of God's fatherhood (vs. 15*a*). He is aware of an aesthetic element in the complexity of the attraction exercised by the nature rituals of paganism (vs. 26). It was obviously not without a struggle that he never worshiped the moon and the stars in their splendor. He also understands the theological meaning of shame in the story of the garden (vs. 33). He is not only a noble man, a specimen of manhood, a civic leader, a benefactor of society, an aesthete, a purist in monotheistic observance. He is also a theologian!

But the worm is in the fruit. The recital of all these achievements and concerns, ethical keenness and social magnanimity, displays the inward vitiation of the perfect man: he has lost the sense of his creatureliness. He will approach God as an equal. Indeed, the prince of the desert will welcome the divine guest, with aristocratic propriety, perhaps with a faint touch of condescendence. "As a prince I shall approach God!" (Vs. 37.)[6] His morality has become the curse of his religion. Rather, his insistence on the power of religion has spoiled his morality. The religious claims of his morality have made his religion null and void. His noblest capacity is the source of his deepest perplexity.

The poet reveals the profundity of his insight when he portrays Job defiant until the end of the discourse. This defiance is both the sign of the hero's virtue and the mark of the hero's crime. Man erects himself as the equal of God. "As a prince, I shall welcome him!" Man's genuine nobility becomes man's curse. Morality has taken the place of ritual, but like ritual it has become a method of forcing heaven. It is a tool for self-deification. Man is always estranged from God when he seeks existential independence. The problem of atheism is really the problem of autonomous humanism.

In a world of social and religious decency, or, as T. S. Eliot expresses it,

> In the land of lobelias and tennis flannels,
> The rabbit shall burrow and the thorn revisit,

[6] Many critics have conjectured that the challenge of God (vss. 35-37) is accidentally displaced. They note, among other details, that the conditional clause, immediately preceding, remains in suspense (vs. 34), while the end of the self-malediction is to be found in verses 38 to 40. They also argue that, after the climactic demand of verses 35 to 37, the resumption of the style of oath-taking with its mention of thistles and cockle constitutes a clear case of bathos. Caution is needed, however, before the text is tampered with, for all Hebrew manuscripts and ancient versions are in agreement on the textual sequence, and ancient rhetoric, especially in the Near East, is different from modern and occidental canons of stylistic elegance. The poet of Job has a predilection for the device of the afterthought and he may also prefer to stress the climactic element not at the end, but in the penultimate instant.

The nettle shall flourish on the gravel court,
And the wind shall say: "Here were decent
    godless people:
Their only monument the asphalt road
And a thousand lost golf balls."[7]

Perhaps the allusion to the thistles and cockle (vs. 40) is climactic, after all. With all the tokens of his generosity, Job is the paragon of refined egotism. With all his care to reject pagan aestheticism in an effort to safeguard the strictest form of monotheism, Job has erected his own self as a god. *Et eritis sicut Dei!* This is the perennial threat to religious moralism. The law is good and must be fulfilled, but in the measure with which it is fulfilled it deteriorates the elemental reality without which man loses the meaning of his own existence—harmony with his creator. Works of morality are like works of piety: unless they follow harmony with God rather than precede it, they foment separation between the divine and the human. Job expects to meet God, but on his own terms. He does worse than to curse God: he makes God unnecessary. At this moment, he in effect capitulates to the orthodoxy of his friends as well as to the heterodoxy of his wife, for the God he summons from the void is the God of ethical satisfaction and ethical recognition. Job wishes to meet God for only one purpose: to obtain a vindication of his rights. But why should he care that God acknowledge his work? There is faith at the very core of his unfaith. Job risks the storms of the true God.

---

[7] "The Word of the Lord Came Unto Me Saying," in *The Rock*, 1934.

Chapter 7

Risking the Storms of God

The Discourses of Elihu the Buzite, 32:1—37:24

NO FIGURE of the Bible has been more often maligned than that of Elihu. Commentators observe that this section of the poem did not originate from the Joban poet himself, and they are probably right. Chapters 32 to 37 display a language and a style which are noticeably different from those of the poetic discussion (chs. 3—31) and of the Lord's discourses (38:1—42:6). For example, the vocabulary of Elihu is strongly flavored with words borrowed from the Aramaic, and many Hebrew verbs are conjugated or constructed in peculiar ways. One might argue that the poet, like Shakespeare or any modern dramatist, could make one of his characters speak in a distinctive fashion, but the question arises at once: Why is the language of the three friends, the hero, and the Lord, identical? Moreover, Elihu's method is different from that of Eliphaz, Bildad and Zophar. He quotes Job verbatim as if he had at his disposal a fixed text (albeit oral) of the poetic dialogue. In all probability, these poetic speeches were contributed by a poet of the Joban school, living in the next

189

generation or even later, who wished to stress one special theme which had been practically ignored in the original poem: the significance of suffering as an educational and revelatory process.

There are passages of great beauty in Elihu's speeches, as well as thoughts of genuine depth. If we pay attention to the original and biblical principle of corporate personality, in literary creation as well as in sociology, we might well try to appreciate the specific contribution of a later poet. We might even be led to recognize in time that the intervention of Elihu fulfills a psychological, dramatic, artistic and theological function. For it prepares the hero—and the reader—for the hearing of the Voice from the Whirlwind. It reveals the love of God under the front of enmity. It points to the reality of salvation by faith. It constitutes a threshold—however imperfect—to the Holy of Holies.

The poems of Elihu are articulated in the following manner:

Introduction in Prose and Verse (32:1-22)
Poem 1: Grace Through an Intercessor (33:1-33)
Poem 2: The Ways of God (34:1-37)
Poem 3: The Giver of Songs in the Night (35:1-16)
Poem 4: The Mercy of the Creator (36:1-25)
Poem 5: The Lord of the Seasons (36:26—37:22)
Conclusion on the Fear of the Lord (37:23-24)

I

Introduction in Prose and Verse, 32:1-22

1. So these three men ceased to answer Job, because he was righteous in his own eyes.

2. Then was kindled the wrath of Elihu the son of Barachel the Buzite, of the kindred of Ram: against Job
was his wrath kindled, because Job justified himself
rather than God.
3. Also against his three friends was his wrath kindled,
because they had found no answer, and yet had condemned Job.
4. Now Elihu had waited till Job had spoken, because
they were older than he.
5. When Elihu saw that there was no answer in the
mouth of these three men, then his wrath was kindled.
6. And Elihu the son of Barachel the Buzite answered;
and he said:

i

I am young in days
  and ye are very old;
therefore I was afraid and durst not
  show you mine opinion.

7. I said, Days should speak,
      and multitude of years should teach wisdom.
8. But there is a spirit in mortal man,
      and the breath of the Almighty giveth him
        understanding.
9. Great men are not always wise:
      neither do the aged understand what is right.
10. Therefore I say, Hearken unto me;
      I also will show you mine opinion.

ii

11. Behold, I waited for your words;
      I gave ear to your reasons,
        whilst ye searched out what to say.
12. Yea, I attended unto you,
      and, behold, there was none of you that con-
        vinced Job,
      or that answered his words:

13. Beware lest ye say, We have found out wisdom:
      God thrusteth him down, not man.
14. Now he hath not directed his words against me:
      neither will I answer him with your speeches.

iii

15. They are amazed, they answer no more;
      they have left off speaking.
16. Shall I wait, because they do not speak?
      because they stand still, and answer no more?
17. I also will answer my part;
      I also will show mine opinion.

18. For I am full of words;
      the spirit within me constraineth me.
19. Behold, my belly is as wine which hath no vent;
      it is ready to burst like new wineskins.
20. I will speak, that I may be refreshed:
      I must open my lips and answer.

21. Let me not, I pray you, show partiality to any man:
      neither let me give flattering titles unto any
      human being!
22. For I know not to give flattering titles;
      else would my Maker soon take me away.

The prose exordus (32:1-5) has preserved a collec-
tion of scribal notices which indicates the complexity of
literary fixation and transmission. Elihu, whose name
means "My God is He," was perhaps conceived as an
Aramean living at the confines of Arabia and Edom.
The name is used for several individuals in Hebrew
history (I Sam. 1:1; I Chron. 12:20; 26:7; 27:18).
Buz is a brother of Uz (Gen. 22:21; cf. Job 1:1) and
an Aramean (Gen. 11:26 ff., etc.); also a locality in
Edom (Jer. 25:23).

The reason for Elihu's intervention is clear: Job has
justified himself rather than God. He has undertaken
to compose an "anthropodicy" rather than a theodicy!
His friends, however, have failed to silence him. Elihu
must refute the hero, and by implication he condemns
the friends.

The tone of the poetic preface (32:6-22) explains
the harshness of the judgments which are generally
passed on Elihu by the exegetes of Job. He is young,
shy, therefore arrogant, also uncouth and decidedly vul-
gar. Since, however, this tone will almost disappear
from the subsequent poems, the author may well have
intended every ludicrous word of the introduction in
order to obtain a comic effect and to relieve the intensity
of the dramatic tension. As Lear staggers in the storm,
Kent asks,

> But who is with him?

and someone answers,

> None but the fool, who labours to outjest
> His heart-struck injuries.

II

Poem 1

Grace Through an Intercessor, 33:1-33

i

33:1. Wherefore, Job, I pray thee, hear my speech,
and hearken to all my words.

2.   Behold, now I open my mouth,
        my tongue in my mouth speaketh.
3.   My words declare the uprightness of my heart,
        and what my lips know they shall utter clearly.
4.   The spirit of God hath made me,
        and the breath of the Almighty hath given
            me life.
5.   If thou canst answer me,
        set thy words in order before me, stand up.
6.   Behold, I am before God exactly as thou art:
        I also am formed out of the clay.
7.   Behold, no dread of me shall make thee afraid,
        neither shall mine hand be heavy upon thee.

ii

8.   Surely thou hast spoken in mine hearing,
        and I have heard the voice of thy words,
            saying,
9.   "I am clean without transgression;
        I am innocent, neither is there iniquity in me.
10. "Behold, he findeth occasions against me,
        he counteth me for his enemy;
11. "He putteth my feet in stocks,
        he marketh all my paths."
12. Behold, in this thou art not right: I will answer
            thee,
        that God is greater than mortal man.

iii

13. Why dost thou strive against him?
        for he giveth not account of any of his
            matters.
14. For God speaketh once, yea twice,
        yet man perceiveth it not.
15. In a dream, in a vision of the night,
        when deep sleep falleth upon men,
        in slumberings upon their bed;

16. Then he openeth the ears of man,
     and affrighteth him with visions,[1]
17. that he may turn man from his iniquity,[2]
     and eradicate[1] pride from a strong man.
18. He keepeth back his soul from the pit,
     and his life from perishing by the sword.

iv

19. Man is chastened also with pain upon his bed,
     and with lasting agony in his bones;
20. So that his life abhorreth bread,
     and his soul dainty meat.
21. His flesh is consumed away, that it cannot be
     seen;
     and his bones that were not seen stick out.
22. Yea, his soul draweth near unto the grave,
     and his life to the destroyers.

v

23. If there be an angel for him,
     one intercessor among a thousand,
     to show unto man his uprightness;
24. Then he is gracious unto him, and saith [unto
     God],
     Deliver him from going down to the pit:
     I have found a ransom;
25. Let his flesh be fresher than a child's;
     let him return to the days of his youthful
     vigor!

vi

26. Thus the intercessor prayeth unto God,
     and God taketh delight in that man,[3]

[1] Hebrew obscure, text uncertain.
[2] With the LXX.
[3] Syntactic construction uncertain.

And he shall see his face with joy;
for he will render unto man his righteousness.

27.   And that man shall sing before men, saying,
I have sinned and perverted that which was
right,
and it was not requited unto me.

28.   He hath redeemed my soul from going into the
pit,
and my life shall see the light.

vii

29.   Lo, God worketh all these things,
twice, three times, with a man,

30.   To bring back his soul from the pit,
that he may be enlightened with the light of
life.

31.   Mark well, O Job, hearken unto me:
hold thy peace, and I will speak.

32.   If thou hast any thing to say, answer me:
speak, for I desire to justify thee.

33.   If not, hearken unto me;
hold thy peace, and I shall teach thee wisdom.

That Elihu's approach is different from that of the orthodox friends appears at once in the way in which he describes the grace of God. He displays a strange combination of bombastic boasting with genuine humility: he knows that on the level of human existence *sub specie Dei* he is not different from Job (vs. 6). This allows him to say clearly to the patient: However dreadful may have been the deeds of God toward thee, God's intention should not be judged. In effect, suffering is a trial. Surely Job is not a perfect man! Elihu refuses to spell out what act of darkness Job may have committed: at least, pride is an offense (vs. 17). Pain chas-

tens (vs. 19). At the extreme moment, an angel, one
among a thousand, will intercede on the behalf of Job
(vss. 23 ff.).

In strophes *v* (vss. 23-25) and *vi* (vss. 26-28), Elihu
develops a whole theology of salvation. As Marianne
Moore aptly puts it, in "The Sycamore,"

There's more than one kind of grace.

Elihu borrows Job's motifs of the mediator-witness-re-
deemer, but he adapts them to his own views. His words
are elliptic but fraught with meaning. Who is this
"intercessor angel"? What is the importance of the
words, "one among a thousand"? We are at a loss to
guess. On the one hand, we must beware of reading
into the text the insight of Christian faith. On the other
hand, just as Job craves for a God-man, so also a Jewish monotheist, meditating on the transcendence of God,
calls for some being who would atone in a priestly way
for human crimes, whatever these may be. Only a
man who has sensed deeply the pathetic element of human inability to achieve good and who has perceived
that love is more powerful than law could be courageous
enough to reverse the trend of his religious environment
and say: the order of events is not conversion, then grace,
finally salvation; but rather, grace, man's response, salvation. Grace is not grace if it depends on man's
achievement.

Thus, the intercessor angel presents himself to God
and says, "I have found a ransom!" (Vs. 24*b*). This is
not the motif of vicarious suffering as it appears in the
Servant's Songs (Isa. 52:13—53:12), but it implies a

divine sharing in man's sorrow and a divine love that takes upon itself the burden of human tragedy. It is the love that forgives and thus moves man to know himself and to repent.

Eliphaz, Bildad and Zophar, like Amos and the Deuteronomist or John the Baptist, preached repentance. Elihu and some of the psalmists, with Hosea and Jeremiah, or Jesus, have probed so deeply into the mystery of evil and love that they have seen the wideness in God's mercy. The first move cannot be accomplished by man, because the consciousness of involvement in evil is not possible unless he already knows himself to be the object of acceptance. Thus, repentance is no longer the tool of salvation: it is the first result thereof. Man cannot say, "I have sinned," unless he has known already that some intercessor, "one among a thousand," has found for him a ransom. His sense of shame arises with his sense of gratitude. This is the reason for which the biblical understanding of guilt has little to do with the modern psychological use of the term. Biblical man knows his guilt only when he knows himself to be accepted. God takes the initiative of "seeing his face with joy," and confers upon him psychological and social integration (vs. 26), which is never man's own but a constantly renewed gift. As a new man, he will of course share with other men his joy of living (vss. 28-30).

Having "Felt now a gust of grace," he can borrow "The wildness to rejoice."[4]

Elihu offers an anticipation of Job's response to the Voice from the Whirlwind, and finds his place within the ranks of all the biblical witnesses to grace as a spring

[4] Richard Wilbur, "John Chrysostom," in *Things of This World* (New York: Harcourt, Brace and Co., 1956).

of self-knowledge without despair, and of conversion
which leads to creative vocation.

III

Poem 2

The Ways of God, 34:1-37

i

34:2. Hear my words, O ye wise men;
     and give ear unto me, ye that have knowledge.
3. For the ear trieth words,
     as the mouth tasteth meat.
4. Let us choose to us what is right:
     let us know among ourselves what is good.

ii

5. For Job hath said, I am righteous:
     and God hath taken away my right.
6. Against my right I am counted a liar;
     my wound is incurable, yet I am without
       transgression.
7. What man is like Job,
     who drinketh up scorning like water?
8. Which goeth in company with the workers of
      iniquity,
     and walketh with wicked men?
9. For he hath said, It profiteth a man nothing
     that he should delight himself with God.

iii

10. Therefore hearken unto me,
     ye men of understanding;

far be it from God, that he should do wickedness;
and from the Almighty, that he should commit iniquity.

11. For the work of a man shall he render unto him,
and cause every man to find according to his
ways.

12. Yea, surely God will not do wickedly,
neither will the Almighty pervert justice.

13. Who hath given him charge over the earth?
or who hath disposed the whole world?

14. If he set his heart upon man,
if he gather unto himself man's breath,

15. All flesh shall perish together,
and man shall turn again unto dust.

iv

16. If now thou hast understanding,
hear this: hearken to the voice of my words.

17. Shall even he that hateth right govern?
and wilt thou condemn him that is just and
mighty?

18. That saith to a king, Thou wicked!
and to princes, Ye ungodly!

19. That accepteth not the persons of princes,
nor regardeth the rich more than the poor;
for they all are the work of his hands?

20. In a moment shall they die,
and the people shall be shaken at midnight,
and pass away:
and the mighty shall be taken away without
human hand.

v

21. For his eyes are upon the ways of man,
and he seeth all his goings.

22. There is no darkness, nor deep shadow,
where the workers of iniquity may hide
themselves.

23.   For he hath not appointed a time[1] for any man
      to enter into judgment with God.
24.   He shall break in pieces mighty men without
      number,
      and set others in their stead.
25.   Therefore he knoweth their works,
      and he overturneth them in the night,
      so that they are destroyed.
26.   He striketh them as wicked men
      in the open sight of others;
27.   Because they turned back from him,
      and would not consider any of his ways:
28.   So that they cause the cry of the poor to come
      unto him,
      and he heareth the cry of the afflicted.

vi

29.   When he giveth quietness, who then can con-
      demn?
      and when he hideth his face, who then can
      behold him?
      whether it be done against a nation, or a man?
30.   That the hypocrite reign not,
      lest the people be ensnared.
31.   Surely it is meet to say unto God,
      I have borne chastisement, I will not offend
      any more:
32.   That which I see not teach thou me:
      if I have done iniquity, I will do no more.
33.   Should he recompense according to thy mind?
      just because thou refusest?
  For thou must choose, and not I:
      therefore speak what thou knowest.

vii

34.   Men of understanding tell me,
      and the wise man that hearkeneth unto me
      saith,

---

[1] Hebrew obscure.

35.   Job hath spoken without knowledge,
        and his words are without wisdom.
36.   My desire is that Job may be tried unto the end,
        because he answereth as wicked men.
37.   For he addeth rebellion unto his sin,
        he clappeth his hands among us,
        and multiplieth his words against God.

The tone of the second poem is harsher than that of
the first. Since Job has not responded to kindness, his
arrogance must be pierced. The pedant takes hold of
the pastor in Elihu who will now do his best to defend
the justice of God's ways. The attacks of Job are quite
unwarranted (vss. 5-9), for God is not after all power-
less, insane, unprincipled. As James Moffatt translates,
"He is no viceroy lording it on earth!" (Vs. 13*a*.) He
shows no partiality to any man. Should not Job confess
that he has spoken without knowledge (vs. 35)? Here
again, Elihu anticipates the response of the hero to the
Voice from the Whirlwind. It will be noticed that although his spirited defense of transcendence makes no
allowance for the mystery of love in God, it does not
commit the gross error of imagining in concrete details
Job's hypothetical immorality. Elihu correctly discerns
the theological nature of Job's *hubris*. He sees the
heroic stature of one who, like Lear,

> Strives in his little world of man to out-scorn
> The to-and-fro conflicting wind and rain. . . .

Elihu, under his youthful aggressiveness, has respect for
Job. He knows that

> The hero is the world-man, in whose heart
> One passion stands for all, the most indulged.[2]

[2] P. J. Bailey, *Festus: Proem*, ll. 114-115.

Because he feels profoundly the holiness and the justice of God, however, he only wishes that Job would humble himself before so great a maker of the world, and confess his willingness to learn from sorrow another kind of nobility—that of creative acquiescence to divine creativity.

IV

Poem 2

The Giver of Songs in the Night, 35:1-16

i

35:2. Thinkest thou this to be right,
    that thou saidst, My righteousness is before God?

3. For thou saidst to him, What advantage will it be unto thee?
    and, What profit shall I have, if I be cleansed from my sin?

4. I will answer thee,
    and thy friends with thee.

ii

5. Look unto the heavens, and see;
    and behold the clouds which are brighter than thou.

6. If thou sinnest, what doest thou against him?
    or if thy transgressions be multiplied, what doest thou unto him?

7. If thou be righteous, what givest thou him?
    or what receiveth he of thine hand?

8. Thy wickedness may hurt a man as thou art;
   and thy righteousness may profit the son of
   man.

iii

9. By reason of the multitude of oppressions, the
   oppressed cry out,
   they shout for help by reason of the arm of
   the mighty.
10. But none saith, Where is God my maker,
    who giveth songs in the night?
11. Who teacheth us more than the beasts of the
    earth,
    and maketh us wiser than the fowls of heaven?
12. There they cry, but none giveth answer,
    because of the pride of evil men.

iv

13. Surely God will not hear vanity,
    neither will the Almighty regard it.
14. Although thou sayest thou dost not see him,
    yet judgment is before him, therefore wait for
    him!
15. But now, because his anger hath not visited,
    and payeth no heed to arrogance,[1]
16. Therefore doth Job open his mouth in vain;
    he multiplieth words without knowledge.

After a new parade of severity in the second poem
(ch. 34), Elihu returns with the third (ch. 35) to an
attitude of conciliation. He has quite shrewdly diag-
nosed Job's error, because he does not stand exactly on
the orthodox position of Eliphaz and the other two
friends. He detects the subtle resemblance that under a

---

[1] *Hapax legomenon;* translation uncertain. The word is probably a cognate
of the verb *púsh*, "to spring out," "to jump up like gamboling calves."

superficial antithesis unites the utilitarian concept of
religion with the attacks of a man who suffers from the
failure of piety (vs. 4). At the same time, the praise of
transcendence should not entail human lawlessness:
while Elihu knows like Eliphaz (22:2 ff.) that God is
independent of man and does not need man's service, he
refuses to admit that there is no pleasure or sorrow in
God over man's behavior (vss. 6-8). As all sufferers are
prone to do, Job has seen in his calamity only the disruptiveness. But there is also in pain and grief a constructive potentiality: if man knows the higher purpose
of the Creator, he ought to endure injury better than the
mass of a bleeding humanity among whom

> None saith, Where is God my maker
> who giveth songs in the night? (Vs. 10.)

Man should use his sorrow in aesthetic creativity.
Music will not release the grip of dread, but it will
transmute its destructive power into creative joy.
There is of course a lyricism which is not prompted by
"the dark struggle of the soul." Moreover,

> Song's breath is wasted when it does but fan
> the smouldering infelicity of man.

But genuine music is born of universal agonies. It must
participate in the parturition of good even among the
damned. Cries the poet,

> Open my ears to music; let
> Me think with Spring's first flutes
> and drums—

> But never let me dare forget
> The bitter ballad of the slums.

Sensitive artists know that

> there are deeds
Which have no form, sufferings which have no tongue,

but they are artists only in so far as they stand under the
tragic curse and break it by expressing it in beauty.
There is no creation without a death, no birth without
pangs, and no music without a measure of identification
in love with the passion of a God who suffers for humanity. It is "God my maker" who "giveth songs in the
night."

Thomas Mann remarked in *Dr. Faustus* that a certain kind of music "needs to be redeemed from pompous
isolation," since "it corresponds to a culture for the elite
which is a substitute for religion." There is also a music
which reflects only the erotic and the heroic, but not the
"givenness," the *agape* love descending from Creator to
creature. When Shelley sings,

> I pant for the music which is divine,
> My heart in its thirst is a dying flower;
> Pour forth the sound like enchanted wine,
> Loosen the notes in a silver shower;

he worships Great God Pan, a deified nature in which
all pantheistic mystics attempt to lose their identity.

Music as escapism is not more biblical than religion as solace; for Job, ahead of that man on his wood, knew

> The parching thirst of death;

And he tried

> The slumb'rous potion bland, [but would] not drink.

Music that lures man to dissolve his will into the "infinity" of a nature christened "God" is the same as pride that pulls him to seek intoxication with love of self; like most forms of piety, it has nothing to do with biblical faith. Music cannot be

> A romantic flight into the ethereal spheres,

because it only channels the response of creature to the "given" of Creator. Like the act of worship as conceived by the psalmists, it does not ascend from man or emerge from his grief or his want. It rather descends from heaven like a dove; it comes down as good news; it refreshes like the rain; it tumbles down with God, very God, self-emptied of his divinity, taking upon his shoulders—he, the Maker of the world and my Maker —the vestments or rather the rags, with mud and blood, of common humanity. Realities remained unadorned. The night is unopened. But in it, the songs are given, even when the hidden God remains silent.

Elihu, for the third time, goes far beyond the theo-

logical limitations of the dialogue. Again he prepares
the climax of the poem in the Voice from the Whirlwind.

V

Poem 4

The Mercy of the Creator, 36:1-25

i

36:2.   Suffer me a little, and I will show thee
   that I have yet to speak on God's behalf.
 3.   I will fetch my knowledge from afar,
   and will ascribe righteousness to my Maker.
 4.   For truly my words shall not be false:
   God that is perfect in knowledge is with thee.

ii

 5.   Behold, God is mighty, and despiseth not any:
   he is mighty in strength and wisdom.
 6.   He preserveth not the life of the wicked;
   but giveth right to the poor.
 7.   He withdraweth not his eyes from the righteous,
   and kings upon the throne he establisheth for
    ever,
   whenever they exalt him.
 8.   But if they be bound in fetters,
   and be holden in cords of affliction;
 9.   Then he showeth them their work,
   and their transgressions, that they have
    exceeded arrogantly their lot.[1]

---

[1] Hebrew *yithgabbârû*, from the root *gâbhar*, a cognate of *gébher*, "strong
man," and of *gibbôr*, "hero," "champion."

10. He openeth also their ear to discipline,
    and commandeth that they return from
    iniquity.

11. If they obey and serve him,
    they shall spend their days in prosperity,
    and their years in pleasures.

12. But if they obey not, they shall perish by the
    sword,
    and they shall die without knowledge.

iii

13. The hypocrites in heart heap up wrath:
    they cry not for help when he bindeth them.

14. They die in youth,
    and their life ends among priests of pagan
    shrines.

15. He delivereth the poor in his affliction,
    and openeth their ears in adversity.

16. Even so would he have allured thee out of the
    strait
    into a broad place, where there is no straitness;
    and that which should be set on thy table
    should be full of butter and cream.

17. But thou hast fulfilled the judgment of the
    wicked;
    judgment and justice shall take hold on thee.

18. Beware lest wrath entice thee away into scoffing:
    then even a great ransom could not deliver thee.

19. Will thy riches keep thee from choking? no, not
    gold,
    nor all the forces of strength.

20. Desire not the night,
    when people are cut off in their place.

21. Take heed, regard not iniquity:
    for this hast thou chosen rather than affliction.

iv

22. Behold, God exalteth by his power:
    who teacheth like him?

23. Who hath enjoined him his way?
     or who can say, Thou hast wrought iniquity?
24. Remember to magnify his work,
     which men praise in song.
25. Every man may see it;
     even mortal man may behold it afar off.

The poetic form of Elihu's discourses gradually changes in such a way that the literary critic has the right to discern in it a sophisticated pattern. Even the prose notices seem to stress a development, from "And Elihu answered" (32:6a and 34:1) to "And Elihu proceeded" (36:1). This change fits the inner growth of the line amplitude, which must be appreciated in the Hebrew original but may even be sensed in the translation. The variations of the strophic structure also point to an acceleration of the speaker's heartbeat, as if he were slowly being grasped by a sense of the holy, which will culminate in the lyricism of the last hymn, immediately before the intervention of the Lord in the storm.

In his fourth poem Elihu continues to reveal that his faith is not static, as were the traditional beliefs of the three friends, but moves beyond rote learning. Admittedly, he falls back at first upon the old idea of poetic justice (vss. 2-7), but while the friends had spoken only of pain in terms of retribution, he stresses the purposes of affliction (vss. 8-12). Also, while the friends had likened Job to a common criminal, Elihu hints that Job resembles the kings who scale the heights (vs. 9). He pays tribute to the greatness of the titan, as if he said in effect:

Grim iron must master you, and shock on shock,
meet the insurrection of your rock,

and with the terrible sculpture of chisels stun

your being till you stand beyond your own
endurance, as if achieved in heroic stone
where marble embodies a god with the vigor of man.[2]

Finally, unlike the friends, he has observed the contradiction which rips Job apart: the struggle from pride
to despair hurls the hero down from an assertion of *hubris* to the courting of death. Elihu warns,

> Do not long for the night (vs. 20*a*),

for life in the underworld is nothing but extinction. Do
not be tempted by the mystery initiations into the nature
cults. The priests of the pagan shrines (vs. 14) with
whom men die of wasted youth are actually the sacred
prostitutes who bring upon the deity's nuptial couch
their desire for immortality. There is only one course
open: participation, through worship, in the work of
the Maker of Life. The last strophe (vss. 22-25) links
the didactic poems with the hymnic exaltation of the
Lord of nature.

VI

Poem 5

The Lord of the Seasons, 36:26—37:22

i

The Ruler of Autumn

36:26. Behold, God is great, and we know him not,
neither can the number of his years be
searched out.

[2] Luke Zilles, "The Marble," from *Conch of Bees.*

27. For he maketh small the drops of water;
    he distilleth his mist into the Autumn rain,
28. Which the clouds at last pour down
    and shower upon the multitudes.
29. Can any one understand the spreading of the
    clouds?
    or the thundering of his tabernacles?
30. Behold, he scattereth his lightning upon it,
    and uncovereth the bottom of the sea.
31. For by them judgeth he the people;
    he giveth meat in abundance.
32. He raiseth the lightning upon the palm of his
    hands;
    and commandeth it to strike the mark.
33. His thunder declareth concerning him
    that he is zealous against iniquity.[1]

ii

37:1. Yea, at this mine heart trembleth,
    and leapeth out of his place.
2. Hear, O hear the crashing of his voice,
    and the roaring that goeth out of his mouth!
3. He directeth it under the whole heaven,
    and his lightning unto the ends of the earth.
4. After it his voice rumbleth:
    he thundereth with the voice of his excel-
    lency;
    and he will not stay the lightnings when his
    voice is heard.
5. God thundereth marvelously with his voice;
    great things doeth he, which we cannot
    comprehend.

iii
The Lord of Winter

6. For he saith to the snow, Be thou on the earth;
    likewise to the showers of drenching rain, Be
    strong.[1]

[1] Hebrew uncertain.

7. Then he sealeth up the working hand of man,
    that every mortal man may know his work.

8. Then the beasts go into their dens,
    and they remain in their lairs.

9. Out of the Austral Chambers cometh the hurri-
    cane,
    and cold from the north winds.

10. By the breath of God frost is given,
    and the breadth of the waters is straitened
    thick with ice.

11. Again with moisture he burdeneth the thick
    cloud;
    and the thunderhead scattereth his light-
    ning.

12. It is turned round about by his counsels,
    that they may do whatsoever he commandeth
    them
    upon the face of the world earthward.

13. He causeth it to come, whether for correction,
    or for his land, or for mercy.

iv

The Lord of Summer

14. Hearken unto this, O Job:
    stand still, and consider the wondrous works
    of God.

15. Dost thou know how God disposeth them,
    and causeth the lightning of his cloud to
    shine?

16. Dost thou know the balancings of the clouds,
    the wondrous works of him which is perfect
    in knowledge?

17. Thou, whose garments are burning hot,
    when he quieteth the earth by the south
    wind?

18. Hast thou with him spread out the vault of the
    sky,
    hard as a molten looking-glass?

19.   Teach us what we shall say unto him;
        for we cannot order our brief by reason of
        darkness.
20.   Shall it be told him that I speak?
        or that a man wisheth he be swallowed up?
21.   And now men cannot look on the light,
        when it is bright in the firmament,
        and a wind hath passed, and cleansed the
        haze away.
22.   Golden weather hath come out of the north:
        with God is terrible majesty.

23.   The Almighty—we cannot find him out;
        excellent in power and in judgment,
        and plenteous in righteousness: he will not
        afflict.
24.   Men do therefore fear him:
        he respecteth not any that are wise in their
        own conceit.

The discourses of Elihu move unceasingly toward a
symphonic finale of praise for the sovereign of nature.
No philosophical solution of the problem of evil has
been sought. Elihu is aware of human finiteness, and
while suffering is a reality which he does not dismiss
lightly, his own life of adoration enables him to lead
Job into the biblical art of contemplation by worship.

The psalmists have brought this art to its highest quality. In the midst of historical strictures hardly paral-
leled in the life of other nations, the singers of Israel
inserted poetic form and theological content into the
exercise of cult. Elihu reflects in his hymn the psalmodic
touch of genius.

There is a time for lament. The dirge is an art form
which confers upon the moan an articulate objectivity

that purges and deflects pain, while using it as a tool of knowledge. It accomplishes much more. It gives body to the response of man before his Maker.

The hymn has another function. It saves from self-pity by turning the self toward participation not in the life of the infinite universe but within the activity of the infinite Being which upholds the finite universe. It attunes man with theocentric harmony, away from anthropocentric discord.

There is no sense of nature in the Bible, according to the popular meaning of the expression. A sense of nature is usually associated with romantic sentimentalism which significantly speaks of Nature (with a capital letter) in religious terms. The aesthetic thrill produced by some of the most beautiful lines in the English language cannot blind us to the fallacy they promote. When we read,

> a sense sublime
> Of something far more deeply interfused,
> Whose dwelling is the light of setting suns,

we know what comes afterwards,

> A motion and a spirit, that impels
> All thinking things, all objects of all thought,
> And rolls through all things. . . .[2]

A sense of nature is only a projection of man's interpretation of life. For many who have endured the torments of a Job, the myth of a communing universe is no longer

[2] William Wordsworth, "Lines Composed a Few Miles Above Tintern Abbey."

a creative symbol, as when Alfred Kreymborg confides
in "Kindred":

> And the woods were hushed and I heard the name
> Of Man in his agony crying aloud,
> And Nature vanished there and then. . . .

Elihu does not ask Job to forget his social and theological isolation by consorting with universal harmon-
ies. He invites him to magnify the Lord of the world.
When faith in a transcending creator is affirmed, nature
is not an end in itself but merely a hint of the intelligent
and mysterious power which moves behind it. Biblical
faith knows that

> The world is charged with the grandeur of God,

and therefore sees that

> There lives the dearest freshness deep down things;

but this vision is possible only

> Because the Holy Ghost over the bent
>   World broods with warm breast and with
>   ah! bright wings.[3]

This mythopoetic language is not to be slighted. Whoever uses it contemplates, like Elihu, not the world but
the personal reality which only gives the world a meaning. The Lord of nature, in the hymn, rules over the
seasons on account of his concern for man. Steadfast

---

[3] Gerard Manley Hopkins, "God's Grandeur."

loyalty to his covenant with mankind is the spring of his creativity (37:13).

From Autumn (36:26-33) and its renewal (in the Near Eastern climate the rebirth of life is not vernal but occurs when the parched soil regains its greenness in November) to Winter (37:1-13) and its torrential or icy interruption of human activity, Elihu's hymn moves up directly to Summer (37:14-22) when the light, the heat and the stillness bring their intimations of mortality. The question is then asked pointedly of Job, in the context of God's embrace of life,

> Shall it be told God . . .
>   that a man wisheth he be swallowed up? (Vs. 20.)

Again the cycle of the year closes. Autumn storms are threatening (vs. 22). Job has been "Risking the Storms of God." Is he ready for a Whirlwind?

Chapter 8

The Irony of Love and Faith

The Discourses of the Lord and Job's Response, 38:1—42:6

A POET must be endowed with either uncommon brashness or with supreme dedication when he presumes to speak in the name of the Deity. The Discourses of the Lord should not be placed in the same category as the oracles of the prophets. These received their words under specific conditions of psychological compulsion, and they were convinced of their own inspiration. A man like the Joban poet, on the contrary, is primarily an artist. This remark does not mean that artists are not inspired, but it does stress the elements of skill, deliberate purposiveness and intellectual reflection in the process of literary composition.

The majority of contemporary critics admit the Joban originality of these poems, although they grant that some strophes and lines have been lengthened in the process of oral transmission, and that the poems themselves have been somewhat overloaded with additional sketches (for example, the description of the ostrich in 39:13-18 and parts of the development on Leviathan in 41:12-34). There is little doubt about the homogeneity

of the Discourses with the Dialogue. Even the folk tale
included some divine intervention (42:7), and Job re-
peatedly called for the manifestation of God (9:2, 3,
14-16, 17, 20, 29-31; 10:6, 7; 13:14-21; etc.). He then
wound up his challenge with the aristocratic self-assur-
ance that the Almighty would comply with his demand.
The fact that the Voice spoke from the Whirlwind and
did not vindicate or explain is no argument in favor of
the conjecture that it is a later addition. Should not the
Deity astonish man's expectation? In any case, charac-
teristics of style, vocabulary and grammar suffice to indicate the same unmistakable hand.

I

The First Discourse of the Lord

Exordium, 38:1-3

38:1.   Then the LORD answered Job out of the whirl-
       wind, and said,
   2.   Who is this that darkeneth counsel
       by words without knowledge?
   3.   Gird up now thy loins like a man:
       for I will demand of thee, and answer thou
       me.

Poem 1

The Creator of the World, 38:4-38

i

   4.   Where wast thou when I laid the foundations
       of the earth?
       declare, if thou hast understanding.

5. Who hath laid the measures thereof, if thou
        knowest?
     or who hath stretched the line upon it?
6. Whereupon are the foundations thereof
        fastened?
     or who laid the corner stone thereof?
7. When the morning stars sang together,
     and all the sons of God shouted for joy?

ii

8. Or who shut up the sea with doors,
        when it brake forth, as if it had issued out of
        the womb?
9. When I made the thunderhead the garment
        thereof,
     and thick darkness a swaddling band for it,
10. And raised for it my decreed limit,
     and set bars and doors,
11. And said, Hitherto shalt thou come, but no
        further:
     and here shall thy proud waves be stayed?

iii

12. Hast thou commanded the morning since thy
        days,
     and caused the dayspring to know his place?
13. That it might take hold of the skirts of the
        earth,
     that the wicked might be shaken out of it?
14. It is turned as red as clay for a seal,
     and it is dyed as a colored vestment.[1]
15. But it withholdeth its light from the wicked,
     that the uplifted arm be broken.

iv

16. Hast thou entered into the springs of the sea?
     or hast thou walked in the recesses of the
        depth?

[1] Hebrew uncertain.

17. Have the gates of death been opened unto thee?
     or hast thou seen the doors of the deep
     shadow?
18. Hast thou perceived the breadth of the earth?
     declare, if thou knowest it all.

v

19. What is the way where light dwelleth?
     and as for darkness, where is the place
     thereof?
20. That thou shouldest take them to the home
     thereof,
     and that thou shouldest know the paths to the
     house thereof?
21. Knowest thou it, because thou wast then born?
     or because the number of thy days is great?

vi

22. Hast thou entered into the treasures of the
     snow?
     or hast thou seen the treasures of the hail?
23. Which I have reserved against the time of
     trouble,
     against the day of battle and war?
24. By what way is the fog parted,
     or where is the east wind scattered upon the
     earth?

vii

25. Who hath divided a watershed for torrential
     rains,
     or a way for the thunderbolt?
26. To cause it to soak the earth, where no man is,
     on the wilderness, wherein there is no man?

27.   To satisfy the desolate and waste ground;
          and to cause the bud of the tender herb to
          spring forth?

viii

28.   Hath the rain a father?
          or who hath begotten the drops of dew?
29.   Out of whose womb came the ice?
          and the hoary frost of heaven, who hath
          gendered it?
30.   The waters are hid as with a stone,
          and the face of the deep is frozen.

ix

31.   Canst thou bind the sweet influences of
          Pleiades?
          or loose the bands of Orion?
32.   Canst thou bring forth the Southern Cross in
          her season?
          or canst thou guide the Great Bear and her
          sons?
33.   Knowest thou the ordinances of heaven?
          canst thou set the dominion thereof in the
          earth?

x

34.   Canst thou lift up thy voice to the clouds,
          that the abundance of waters may obey thee?[2]
35.   Canst thou send forth lightnings, that they may
          go,
          and say unto thee, Here we are?
36.   Who hath put wisdom in the ibis,
          or who hath given understanding to the
          cock?[3]

[2] Hebrew uncertain.
[3] The translations "ibis" and "cock" are conjectural: the former is the
bird of Thot, the Egyptian god of wisdom, which announced the flood of
the Nile; the latter announces morning.

37.   Who can number the clouds in his wisdom,
        or who can title the waterskins of heaven?[4]
38.   When the dust groweth into hardness,
        and the clods cleave fast together?

Poem 2

The Lord of the Animals, 38:39—39:30

i

38:39.   Wilt thou hunt the prey for the lion?
            or fill the appetite of the young lions,
40.   When they couch in their dens,
        and abide in the covert to lie in wait?
41.   Who provideth for the raven his food?
        when his young ones cry unto God,
        and wander for lack of meat?

ii

39:1.   Knowest thou the time when the wild goats of
            the rock bring forth?
            or canst thou mark when the hinds do calve?
2.   Canst thou number the months that they fulfil?
        or knowest thou the time when they bring
            forth?
3.   They bow themselves, they bring forth their
            young ones,
        they cast out their sorrows.[4]
4.   And when their offspring hath waxed strong,
        they go forth, and return not to them.

iii

5.   Who hath sent out the wild ass free?
        or who hath loosed the bands of the onager;
6.   Whose house I have made the wilderness,
        and the barren land his dwellings?

4 Hebrew uncertain.

7. He scorneth the multitudes of the city,
    neither regardeth he the shouting of the
    driver.
8. The range of the mountains is his pasture,
    and he searcheth out every green thing.

iv

9. Will the buffalo be willing to serve thee?
    or abide by thy crib?
10. Canst thou bind the wild ox with his band in
    the furrow?
    or will he harrow the valleys after thee?
11. Wilt thou trust him, because his strength is
    great?
    or wilt thou leave thy labor to him?
12. Wilt thou believe him, that he will bring home
    thy seed?
    and gather it into thy threshing floor?

v

13. Gavest thou the wings unto the ostrich?
    They are not like those of the stork or hawk,[5]
14. But she leaveth her eggs in the earth,
    and warmeth them in the dust,
15. And forgetteth that the foot may crush them,
    or that the wild beast may break them.
16. She is hardened against her young ones,
    as though they were not hers:
    she laboreth in vain but is without fear.
17. Because God hath deprived her of wisdom,
    neither hath he imparted to her understand-
    ing.

[5] Hebrew uncertain.

18.   Yet, when she lifteth up herself on high,
      she scorneth the horse and his rider.

vi

19.   Hast thou given the horse strength?
      hast thou clothed his neck with thunder?[6]
20.   Canst thou make him afraid as a grasshopper?
      the glory of his snorting is terrible.
21.   He paweth in the valley, and rejoiceth in his
      strength:
      he goeth on to meet the armed men.
22.   He mocketh at fear, and is not affrighted;
      neither turneth he back from the sword.
23.   The quiver rattleth against him,
      the glittering spear and the shield.
24.   He swalloweth the ground with fierceness and
      rage:
      neither can he stand still at the sound of the
      war horn.
25.   At each trumpet blast he saith, Ha, ha!
      and he smelleth the battle afar off,
      the thunder of captains and the shouting.

vii

26.   Is it by thy wisdom that the hawk soareth,
      and stretch her wings toward the south?
27.   Is it at thine order that the eagle flieth up,
      and make her nest on high?
28.   She dwelleth and abideth on the rock;
      Upon the crag of rock is her aerie.
29.   From thence she seeketh her prey,
      and her eyes behold afar off.

[6] The word "thunder" probably means "trembling one" or "mane." Cf.
the Greek *phobe*, "mane," and *phobos*, "fear."

30.   Her young ones also suck off blood:
       and where the slain are, there is she.

Poem 3

The First Challenge of the Lord to Job, 40:1-5

40:1.   Moreover the LORD answered Job and said,
   2.   Shall he yield, that contendeth with the Al-
         mighty?
         he that reproveth God, let him give an an-
         swer!
   3.   Then Job answered the LORD, and said,
   4.   Behold, I am of small account; what shall I
         return unto thee?
         I will lay mine hand upon my mouth.
   5.   Once have I spoken, and I will not answer:
         yea, twice; and I will proceed no further.

Let us admit that the irony of God is bewildering. It is not even an especially delicate species of sarcasm. Are those interpreters right, therefore, who claim that the Lord scoffs at Job on his pile of manure in a way more reminiscent of a devil than suggestive of a father?

At the extremity of human destitution, Job has implored, begged and demanded that God come and answer the riddle of crucifixion. A derelict of society and a heretic on the verge of excommunication asks for recognition and what does he get? Questions, all of them apparently irrelevant. Has the poet intended to show the irony of love or the irony of hate? Worse, the irony of unconcern?

The motif of the Whirlwind is not in itself significant: it was in all probability inherited from the ancient prose story. While it tends to create an atmosphere of

awe, it is part and parcel of the literary form of eschato-
logical theophany: the appearance of the judge at the
end of history (see Isa. 29:6; 40:24; 41:16; Jer. 23:19;
30:23; Ezek. 1:4; Zech. 9:14; cf. Hab. 3:14; etc.). The
word *se'ārāh* designates no ordinary tempest or thunder-
storm, hurricane or tornado, but the theological setting
of God's manifestation at the end of the world. Incidentally, the use of the term "theophany" here as elsewhere in the Old Testament is improper since the Lord
does not appear in the sense of being seen, but only
speaks from the pitch black of doom, unlighted by the
flashes of fire as on Mount Sinai. What counts is the
poetry, not of the background, but of the words uttered
by the Voice. Those words make excellent Hebrew
lyricism, but is this an added touch of irony? The humor
is "dark" indeed, as the first question to emerge from
the deepest gloom asks,

Who is this that darkeneth counsel? (38:2*a.*)

Job might easily outsmart the divine humorist by re-
torting: And who has the right to speak of darkness,
anyway? Then, the Deity proceeds to expatiate—at some
length—on his creative activity. The poet intends to
bring Job, through some mordant *via negativa,* by a
kind of weird vicariousness, into God's own creative
savoir-faire.

God does not even start as politely as Eliphaz did at
the beginning of the dialogue. He dispenses with the
human pretenses of civility. He does not inquire into
Job's feelings. "And how is the patient today?" God
does not sympathize, does not commiserate, does not
even draw out the sufferer's eagerness to describe symp-

toms of his misery. God does not attempt to understand.
God does not comfort. But he does not patronize either.
He merely commands:

> Gird up now thy loins like a man! (Vs. 3a.)

Here is at last Job's hour, his moment of truth. But first
he must endure an endless sequence of questions which
to modern ears sound like a fantastic parody of the
Negro spiritual,

> Were you there when they crucified my Lord?

Again and again God asks questions, with all the verve
of a cosmic troubadour, and with the seeming irresponsibility of a clown with sad, whitened face:

> Were you there when I laid the foundations of
>   the earth?

Only when we reach the end of the first strophe do we
perceive an altogether different kind of undertone, as if
God himself were caught with divine nostalgia when he
remembers the first dawn:

> When the morning stars sang together,
>   and all the sons of God shouted for joy (vs. 7).

Still, what kind of God is this, who has nothing to say
about Job's torture, or the infants of men, maimed and
unwanted in peace, dying of cold and horror in war?
Job knows that their prayers remain unanswered. Why
should he be forced to hear lessons in geology, astron-

omy, meteorology and zoology, while he is consumed by disease and unrequited love?

God's inexhaustible energy is matched only by his eloquence. In turn, he pictures the settling of the earth upon its base, the shutting up of the sea within its bounds, the waking of "Dawn"—a little godchild, crimson as the clay of Lemnos which men use with their seals— who shakes the wicked like parasites out of earth's night robe.

Of course, Job has not descended, as the goddess Ishtar, through the ten gates of hell, nor could he grasp the secrets of the snow and hail, sirocco or north wind. Even less could he delineate the family affairs of the constellations or summon lightnings at a flash, so to speak. Would he then care to tame all the wonders of God's bestiary? Would he like to spy upon the homes and mores of lionesses and goats, ravens and wild asses? Would he take a fancy to the domestication of the Asiatic buffalo? How about a unicorn for the humble toils of husbandry?[7] He might have an eye for the speed of the senseless ostrich and the courage of the Cilician horse. Would he like to see eaglets sucking blood from prey brought up to their aeries?

Is that truly all that God wants to say to a dying man? Is the heart of the matter only a show of omnipotence against the puniness of humans?

Shall he yield, that contendeth with the Almighty? (40:2a.)

What else could he do? (40:3-5.) Of course, Job will

---

[7] While the time-honored rendering of "unicorn" for "wild ox" (39:9-10) is not scientifically tenable, it may be retained for the simple reason that the mind of classical antiquity did not distinguish rigorously between animals of myth and animals observed.

"proceed no further." Then, is the crushing of a moth the poet's answer to the scandals of human existence?

Job's silencing, however, is only transitional to the second discourse.

II

The Second Discourse of the Lord

40:6—42:6

40:6. Then answered the LORD unto Job out of the whirlwind, and said,

i

7. Gird up thy loins now like a man:
    I will demand of thee; declare thou unto me.
8. Wilt thou even reduce to nought my righteousness?
    Wilt thou condemn me, that thou mayest be justified?
9. Hast thou an arm like God?
    or canst thou thunder with a voice like him?
10. Deck thyself now with majesty and excellency;
    and array thyself with glory and beauty.

ii

11. Cast abroad the rage of thy wrath:
    and behold every one that is proud, and abase him.
12. Look on every one that is proud, and bring him low;
    and tread down the wicked in their place.
13. Hide them in the dust together;
    and bind their faces in the secret place.

14. Then will I also confess unto thee
       that thine own right hand can save thee.

iii

15. Behold, Behemoth,
       which I made as I made thee:
       he eateth grass as an ox.
16. Lo, now, his strength is in his loins,
       and his force is in the muscles of his belly.
17. He stiffeneth his tail like a cedar:
       the sinews of his stones are wrapped together.
18. His bones are as strong pieces of brass;
       his legs are like bars of iron.

iv

19. He is the chief of the ways of God:
       let him who made him bring near his sword!
20. Surely the mountains bring him forth food,
       where all the beasts of the field play.
21. He lieth at ease under the bushes of lotus,
       in the covert of the reeds, and fens.
22. The screens of lotus cover him with their
         shadow;
       the willows of the brook compass him about.
23. Behold, he drinketh up a river, and hasteth not:
       he trusteth that he can draw up Jordan into
         his mouth.
24. Can one take him by [throwing mud] in his
         eyes?[1]
       or pierce his nose with harpoons?

v

41:1. And Leviathan! Canst thou draw him out with
         a hook?
       or press down his tongue with a cord?

[1] Allusion to a hunting method of blinding the hippopotamus with clay
(see Herodotus, *History*, II, 70).

2. Canst thou knot a rope around his nose?
     or bore his jaw through with a thorny stick?
3. Will he make many supplications unto thee?
     will he speak unto thee soft words?
4. Will he make a covenant with thee?
     wilt thou take him for a servant forever?
5. Wilt thou play with him as with a bird?
     or wilt thou put him on leash for thy maidens?

vi

6. Will he be placed on sale by the fishing party?
     shall they cut him apart among the
          merchants?
7. Canst thou fill his skin with barbed irons?
     or his head with fish spears?
8. Lay thine hand upon him;
     remember the battle; do no more.
9. Behold, the hope of men is in vain:
     shall not one be cast down even at the sight of
          him?
10. None is so fierce that dare stir him up:
     who then is able to stand before me?

vii

11. Who hath gone ahead of me, that I should repay
          him?
     whatsover is under the whole heaven is mine.
12. I will not conceal his parts,
     nor his power, nor his comely proportion.
13. Who can uncover his outer garment?
     or who can penetrate his double coat of mail?
14. Who can open the doors of his face?
     Terror is round about his teeth.

viii

15. His scales are his pride,
     shut up together as with a close seal.
16. One is so near to another,
     that no air can come between them.

17. They are joined one to another,
    they stick together, that they cannot be
      sundered.
18. By his sneezings a light doth shine,
    and his eyes are like the eyelids of dawn.
19. Out of his mouth go flaming torches,
    and sparks of fire leap out.
20. Out of his nostrils goeth smoke,
    as out of a seething pot on a rush fire.
21. His breath kindleth coals,
    and a flame goeth out of his mouth.

ix

22. In his neck remaineth strength,
    and terror whirleth before him.
23. The flakes of his flesh are joined together:
    they are firm in themselves; they cannot be
      moved.
24. His heart is hard as a stone;
    yea, as hard as a piece of the nether millstone.
25. When he raiseth up himself, the gods are afraid,
    at his crashing they are beside themselves.

x

26. The sword of him that layeth at him cannot
    hold:
    the spear, the dart, nor the habergeon.
27. He esteemeth iron as straw,
    and brass as rotten wood.
28. The arrow cannot make him flee:
    sling stones are turned with him into stubble.
29. Darts are counted as reeds:
    he laugheth at the shaking of a spear.

xi

30. His underparts are like sharp potsherds:
    he spreadeth himself like a threshing sledge
      on the mire.

31. He maketh the deep to boil like a pot;
    he maketh the sea like a pot of ointment.
32. He leaveth a shining wake after him:
    one would think the deep to be hoary.
33. Upon earth there is not his like:
    a creature without fear.
34. He beholdeth all things:
    he is a king over all the sons of pride.

xii

42:1. Then Job answered the LORD and said,
  2. I know that thou canst do every thing,
    and that no purpose of thine can be thwarted.
  3. [Thou saidst,] Who is this that hideth counsel
      without knowledge?
    Therefore, have I uttered that I understand
      not;
    things too wonderful for me, which I knew
      not.
  4. [Again, thou saidst,] Hear and I will speak;
    I will demand of thee, and declare thou unto
      me.
  5. I had heard of thee by the hearing of the ear;
    but now mine eye seeth thee.
  6. Wherefore I abhor myself,
    and repent in dust and ashes.

As if the first display of divine majesty had not succeeded in producing its intended aim, the Deity renews
the challenge. Job's silence is apparently not deemed
sufficient. To use the terminology of the Middle Ages,
his attrition must become a contrition. He has responded
to God's probing, but only in a negative fashion: by

promising silence. This is no indication that he has
yielded at all. As Albert Camus says in *The Fall* :

His silence is deafening. It's the silence of the primeval
forest, heavy with threats.

Or rather, Job's refusal to continue overtly the struggle
may suggest that he has merely acknowledged the over-
whelming crush of power. His silence does not reveal
his secret attitude toward God. He may have interpreted
the irony of God as an irony of hate. The drama of the
encounter must continue awhile longer, until Job, by
faith, sees in the irony of God an irony of love.

Perhaps the words of the first strophe in the second
discourse of the Lord are among the most significant of
the poem. Asks God of Job,

> Wilt thou reduce to nought my righteousness?
> wilt thou condemn me that thou mayest be
>   justified? (40:8.)

Job has indeed placed the righteousness of God in
doubt. But the tone of the divine speaker has subtly
changed. A deep melancholy underlines the two
phrases. God does not condemn Job, but the poet succeeds in intimating with the eloquence of restraint the
theological character of man's sinfulness. The effort to
justify the ways of man always leads man to condemn
the ways of God. Man trespasses the limits of his humanity whenever he dares to judge the character of the
divinity. Nevertheless, God does not condemn Job, as
Eliphaz and his friends have done, for crimes of morality which Job has not committed. He does not even
chide him, as Elihu would have done, for refusing to

discern in suffering a welcome means of crystal purification. Still more extraordinary, he does not even censure
him for a theological offence which Job *did* commit.
Although he knows, as we do, that Job has raised himself to an heroic stature by swelling his smallness into a
magnitude of divine proportions, God never reproves
him for his *hubris*. The poet's conception of the divinity is far removed from those of Homer and the Greek
tragics. There is no hint in the Lord's Discourses of
any godly envy for Job's prosperity, jealousy for his
happiness, or fear for his exceeding all bounds of measure. Yahweh is not an Olympian Zeus. Job is not a
Prometheus. But the poet unerringly conveys the "beyondness" of the divine Being. It is not God who condemns: it is only man who condemns himself when he
knows God truly as God.

Job has doubted the righteousness of his Creator. At
the same time, he has paradoxically recognized it was
there, since he made claims upon it. But by expecting
from God a vindication of his own righteousness, he
negated the freedom of that God. He condemned God
to human finiteness in an attempt to justify himself. He
conceived divine justice, not in relation to a God-revolv-
ing macrocosm but as a function of his self-centered
microcosm. He denied the theocentricity of the universe
by living anthropocentrically. Had he had the power of
a God, he could have saved himself, and God would have
indeed recognized that man can be the author of his
salvation. The power of man, however vast within the
limited sphere of his mortality, is bound by the ocean of
nothingness. Let Job try to exercise his power abroad
and within, and he will soon discover the weakness of his
right hand (40:11-14).

Thus the experiment has to be resumed, like a forest fire which seems to have spent itself and suddenly flares up in the hidden growth. The divine irony becomes in the second discourse heavier than in the first. Behemoth and Leviathan are the caricatures of the deep. They are much more than the Egyptian hippopotamus and crocodile respectively, although they both draw from their resemblance with those beasts a reputation for abnormal but still nonmetaphysical grossness. They are mythical creatures, projected on the screen of cosmic imagination, but since they are described from the point of view of God, their monstrosity becomes only the subject of comic exaggeration. There is a Gargantuan flavor in this couplet, among several others,

Behold, he drinketh up a river, and hasteth not:
    he trusteth that he can draw up the Jordan into his
    mouth (41:23).

God reveals himself as the genial artist enamored of his work. He both admires and teases the beastly wonders, not only because they scare mercantile hunters out of their wits but also because they are "fearfully and marvelously made." The Lord communes with his creation. For him it is still the first morning with joy unadulterated. Moreover, the poet's imagination hovers among various levels of image associations. These brutish creatures are not only caricatures in themselves; they are also caricatures of human endeavor. Behemoth and Leviathan are not for God the personifications of evil: they are pictures of useless fantasy, and thus they become the symbols of God's freedom. He merely toys with them (Ps. 104:26). Job is scared when the crocodile sneezes and he cannot tie a dainty knot through its nostrils; God, on his side, refuses to throw such freaks as Behemoth and Leviathan out of this world. The mover of the spheres and the ruler of time is endowed with the curiosity and the enjoyment of a child.

God does not condemn Job, because he respects Job's curiosity. In *War in Heaven,* Charles Williams depicts the following exchange between Mornington and the Archdeacon:

"Would you say any kind of curiosity was wrong? What about Job?"

"Job?" the Archdeacon asked.

"Well, sir, I always understood that where Job scored over the three friends was in feeling a natural curiosity why all those unfortunate things happened to him. They simply put up with it, but he, so to speak, asked God what He thought He was doing."

The Vicar shook his head. "He was told he couldn't understand."

"He was taunted with not being able to understand— which isn't quite the same thing," Mornington answered. "As a mere argument there's something lacking perhaps in saying to a man who's lost his money and his house and his family and is sitting on the dustbin, all over boils, 'Look at the hippopotamus.' "

"Job seemed to be impressed," the Archdeacon said mildly.

"Yes," Mornington admitted. "He was certainly a perfect fool, in one meaning or other of the words."

Modern readers may think that God disported himself with calculated dilettantism, and Job may at first have shared this view, but he soon came to disagree with himself.

For after the seeming irrelevancies on Behemoth and Leviathan have run their course, the silent man speaks again, not only to confess his rashness (42:3) and to acknowledge omnipotence (42:1), but also to declare the discovery of his own birth to existence,

> I have heard of thee by the hearing of the ear,
>   but now mine eye seeth thee (42:5).

The allusion to visual perception should not lead us to believe that there was indeed a theophany in the full sense of the word or that the Lord's appearance imprinted its shape of dazzling light upon the patient's retina. Hebrew usage as well as the immediately preceding context (vs. 5a) shows precisely what the poet had in mind: an antithesis between the traditional belief by hearsay, inherited through the intellect from a past now dead, and the actual experience, as piercing as burning coals, as real as death, as warm as life. Job has left the mediacy of belief for the immediacy of faith. The presence he has been seeking is now a proximate actuality. At once, the joy of communion enlightens his faculty of knowledge: the irony of the Lord was moved by love.

Of course, the Lord did not vindicate Job's ethical purity! What a paltry satisfaction it would have been in comparison with the fullness of his grace. The whole perspective is thrown into focus. Questions are no longer asked of man, because questions are no longer asked of God. Existence is fulfilled when man is aware, not of his ultimate concern but of becoming the concern of the ultimate. The derelict knows himself to be accepted by the creator of the universe; the orphan discovers the heart of a father; God's lonely man is received into the society of God.

Precisely at this moment, the pride of the giant has been pulverized, and the sense of his sin engulfs him into self-condemnation. The meaning of the verb usually rendered "I abhor myself" (vs. 6*a*) may never be known. The ancient versions, however, and the possible cognates of the Hebrew root in other Semitic languages probably suggest the idea of "melting," "dissolving," or "sinking," even into an abyss of fall and death. His ego having surrendered, Job's will to react has disintegrated and the only course left for him is to "repent in dust and ashes" (vs. 6).

The word translated "repent" is not the typical Hebrew verb *shûbh*, "to return," hence "to convert oneself" or "to repent."[2] The word used by Job is *nācham*. It denotes the inner motivation of the outward step which leads to "repentance." It means: being moved to deep pathos, to suffer grievous sorrow, especially over one's own deed or behavior.

Awareness of sin comes only to one who is being reconciled. A new despair may grow out of the sense of unworthiness, but it cannot overwhelm, for love is assured. This despair is vitalized into decision.

The surrender is not a mere giving up of self-righteousness. It is an acceptance of sharing in the righteousness of God.

We yeeld, Great Lord, Thou hast subdued us quite,
And unto Thee belongs e'en our self-right.[3]

The new despair arises precisely because we are men

Who fear the blessing of God, the loneliness of the
      night of God,
   the surrender required, the deprivation inflicted;

---

[2] Cf. the Hebrew and Jewish teaching on *Teshûbhāh*, repentance, which greatly influenced the New Testament stress on *metanoia*, "renewal by return."

[3] Joseph Beaumont.

Who fear the injustice of man less than the justice of
    God;
Who fear the hand at the window, the fire in the
    thatch,
  the fist in the tavern, the push in the canal,
Less than we fear the love of God.[4]

Man shrinks from the return, even when he senses the
true intentions which are manifested toward him. The
Lord has not justified Job, but he has come to him in
person. And this means love. Every time man senses
God's love, when it is truly God's love and not a senti-
mental sweetening of the human variety, "it's such an
odd sort of mercy, it sometimes looks like a punishment.[5]
A God who concerns himself for man is a God who
loves. There is no love without sharing and a God who
loves is a God who suffers. Underneath the high notes
a *De Profundis* of God's own agonies is audible.

In vain can man attempt to penetrate through the
scandal of his existence into the heart of the divine
mystery which is Existence itself. Yet, because the Lord
speaks to Job from the Whirlwind, and while darkness
still shrouds his person, Job "sees" him. "The Absolute
power is for human personality's sake become personality.... He offers Himself to him as an answer.[6] Helen
Waddell portrays Peter Abelard quoting to himself the
answer of Job:

This very day he had challenged Heaven to show him
wherein he had sinned; and heaven's answer had been
to show him itself. His righteousness he had held fast

---

4 T. S. Eliot, *Murder in the Cathedral.*
5 Graham Greene, *The End of the Affair.*
6 Martin Buber, *The Prophetic Faith.*

and would not let it go: it lay about him now, like farm-
yard trampled snow.

The self-abhorrence or the sinking sensation is only a
manifestation of reluctance to rebirth and of unworthiness to grace. Emily Dickinson's dialogue portrays this
truth:

> "I am spotted."
> "I am Pardon."
> "I am small."
> "The least
> Is esteemed in Heaven
> The chiefest.
> Occupy my house."

III

Many might wish that Job had spelled out his reticence. However, far from accusing the poet of literary
sterility, we should praise him for keeping the response
of Job to this bare declaration. In the presence of the
holy, Job could not speak. "To make the relation to
God into a feeling is to relativize and psychologize it.
True relation is a *coincidentia oppositorum*, an absolute
which gathers up the poles of feeling into itself."[7] Only
Job's reticence could fit the recipiency of grace. Gabriel
Marcel entered in his Journal on March 5, 1925, the day
of his "conversion":

For the first time I have clearly experienced grace.
A terrible thing to say, but so it is. I am hemmed in at

[7] Maurice S. Friedman, *Martin Buber, The Life of Dialogue.*

last by Christianity—in, fathoms deep. Happy to be so, I will write no more.[8]

Job's response to God's offer of self provides us now with a retrospective view of the meaning of irony as a device of revelation. Job was raised from the narrowness of his outlook to the breadth of God's own horizon. The Deity in Second Isaiah is likewise asking Israel in her straits:

> Lift up your eyes on high and see:
> Who created these? (Isa. 40:26.)

By issuing this admonition, biblical men are not attempting to prove the existence of God. Rather, they are stimulating a sense of wonder for the spirit-swept universe. It is easy to become blasé, even from sorrow, and to brush off holy things as if they were specks of dust on one's lapel, to see the traces of an angel's wing and to mistake it for a psychological mood. It is tempting for us as for the best-selling "Inspirationalist" in James Thurber's fable, to "drag God to the people's level," and to say in effect, "You can be Jehovah's Pal: Have comfy chats with the Lord in the little cozy corners of spare time!" Even without falling into this fashionable cheapening of God in an effort to make faith intelligible to the masses, we know that to become familiar with holiness is to deny it. In the meantime, professionals of "religion" as well as secularists spend their existence in

8 Quoted by T. V. Langmead Casserley, in *Christianity and the Existentialists,* ed. by Carl Michalson.

peripheral pursuits. John Holmes wrote in *The Double Root*:

> And new day upon new day makes earth older,
> Birds dying in migration, trees turned
> Bronze, on seven seas tide turned, turned.
> Else why this sunblown immeasurable height
> Unspeaking? Why this mapped shore not moved?

But mark the poet's rejoiner:

> Only the day man marvels at is saved.

At the root of their creative urge philosophers and scientists, like poets and musicians, need just this—a sense of wonder. Van Wyck Brooks notes that the artist has to receive "the fresh heart that can be surprised by things," or, as Ortega y Gasset puts it, that gift of "looking at the world with eyes wide open in wonder." Even more so the man who thinks on existence. He should have what painters describe as "the innocence of the eye," but this does not mean at all that he should be a starry-eyed innocent. For the biblical sense of wonder is to be sharply distinguished from its pagan counterpart. If we are sensitive to the mystery and the beauty of nature, we must constantly remember that our wonderment at the world has only a penultimate quality. There is a paradoxical similarity between Renaissance humanism and Romantic pantheism: both have led in our time to a certain brand of existentialism which says, with a character of Paul Claudel:

> *N'avons-nous point un droit*
> *A ne point voir Dieu? et je ne puis l'exclure.*

Some of us, by temperament and training, are apt to stress human values and, therefore, practical organiza-

tion based upon scientific technology. As a result of this
"good," we live as if the world of the ballade of Rolfe
Humphries had indeed come to pass:

> There are no wonders any more.
> Energy equals M C square,
> And two and two are always four,
> And who are we to think we care?
> All the enchantments, old and rare,
> Are runes we cannot read; forlorn
> Under persimmon-tree, or pear,
> We've never seen a unicorn.

At the opposite pole, there are others among us who too
readily admit that we are surrounded by an awesome
mystery which our little formulae are inadequate to ex-
press. But those who think thus usually fall from the
Scylla of humanism into the Charybdis of pantheism.
They confuse God with nature just as the others confuse
God with man. "O Nature," Seneca confesses, "how we
worship thee even against our wills." And in *King Lear,*
Edmund exclaims,

> Thou, nature, art my goddess;
> To thy law my services are bound.

And thus we dismiss Easter for springtime and the resurrection for immortality. Such forms of pantheism are
in fact a perversion of humanism, for they imply, with
all mystics of the nonbiblical persuasion, that man is
capable of infinity. But, as Abraham Heschel recalls it:

It is not the sublime as such of which the Biblical man
is aware. To him, the sublime is but a way in which
things react to the presence of God. It is never an ulti-

mate aspect of reality, a quality meaningful in itself. It stands for something greater; it stands in relation to something beyond itself that the eye can never see.

The sublime is not simply there. It is not a thing, a quality, but rather a happening, an act of God, a marvel.... There are no sublime facts; there are only divine *acts.*[9]

The sense of wonder, in the end, is insufficient. It is contemplation of God at work which is called for, and this is exactly what the Discourses of the Lord achieve. They transmute existence into worship by creative participation in the creativity of God.

Worship is not a power-tapping technique for feeling better. It is looking at the only marvel: God the creator of the world and the re-creator who dwells in a broken and contrite heart.

In *contemplation*, if the word can be salvaged from quietistic abuse, there is the reality of divine presence as in a *temple*. Inserted within the living body of the world of men is the *'Am Qādhôsh,* or "holy people," whose calling arose from Abraham's existential decision to uproot himself and to go out on the road, whose mission is the enlightenment and the "salting" of the estranged, and whose end is the reconciliation of man within himself and to his Creator through an awareness of his true home.

Perhaps Ralph Marcus is right when he concludes that the poem of Job offers a peculiar kind of *Imitatio Dei*: not quite "an exhortation to emulate God's unconquerable will,"[10] but a renewal of man's dying nature into the vehicle of creative grace.

[9] Abraham Heschel, *God in Search of Man: a Philosophy of Judaism* (New York: Farrar, Straus & Cudahy, 1955), p. 40.
[10] "Job and God," *The Review of Religion*, Vol. XIV (1949-1950, p. 29.

Participation in the creative work of the Deity does
not remove from existence the enigma and the throbbing
ache.

> I tell you naught for your comfort,
>   Yea, naught for your desire,
> Save that the sky grows darker yet
>   And the sea rises higher.

These lines of John Donne cannot be branded as spring-
ing from pessimism. They depict a man who has reached
a certain stage of maturity in which there is no longer
room for the agony of meaninglessness. The irony of
God's love is matched by the irony of man's faith.

Faith attaches itself to a God who is beyond experience because he stands beyond good and evil as man can
imagine them. Faith is not sight or reason which end
in doubt. Faith takes doubt within itself as it also ab-
sorbs morality. It merely answers grace. "The Law,"
said Pascal, "demands what it cannot give; grace gives
all it demands." Thus it has been correct to affirm that
biblical faith rests not on a theology of man but on an
anthropology of God.

Because the Joban poet foreshadows the theology of
the agony of God, by which human agony is shared and
borne, his poem can transfigure the perplexity of existence into the will to live triumphantly.

Job's first act, after the surrender—and this detail
constitutes probably the poet's single interference with
the epilogue (42:10)—was to intercede on behalf of his
friends. He did not ask for the deliverance of self. He
begged for mercy toward other men.

To him, as he was spying on the Behemoth and the

Leviathan of our lives, W. H. Auden might have addressed the summons:

Follow Him through the Land of Unlikeness;
You will see rare Beasts, and have unique adventures.[11]

By participation with the creating of life, the poet explains nothing, but through his vision, all things are livable.

Job is the poet, hence the prophet, of existence. His poem is neither a treatise nor a masque nor a tragedy. It is a ceremony of sacramental participation in creativity through which the sense of the holy does not paralyze but quickens one to action.

An atheist, like the Roman poet Catullus in Thornton Wilder's *The Ides of March,* cannot be redeemed from his self-centeredness by creativity. Speaking to Clodia Pulcher, his former mistress, who wanted to die with him, Catullus says: "I cannot drown with you, because I have one thing left to do. I can still insult this universe which insults us. I can insult it by making a beautiful thing. That I shall do; and then, I shall put an end to the long crucifixion of the mind." Creativity must transcend aesthetics: or else, it is a perversion of the love of life into the love of self.

Job is the poet of existence, because he sinks into the abyss only when he has tasted the fullness of creative concern. His fascination for nothingness is overcome exactly as his dread of death. He has traveled a world beyond the ignorance and the arrogance of religion. Risking the storms of God, he finds in the divine irony

[11] "The Flight into Egypt," Part IV, from *The Time Being, A Christmas Oratorio* (New York: Random House).

a hint of love to which he responds by the irony of faith, which sees while not seeing, and lives by not refusing to die.

"Vitality," wrote Paul Tillich in *The Courage to Be*, "is the power of creating beyond oneself without losing oneself." And this is precisely what Job learns from the active contemplation of God's creativity. He becomes alive with the mover of the world,

> when the morning stars sing together,
> and the sons of God shout for joy.

Poets, scientists, novelists, dramatists, painters, sculptors, architects, musicians, all those who create with the stuff of human life; mothers and fathers, teachers and counselors, physicians and all those who mediate life to their children or neighbors—these discover the meaning of existence in the miracle of creativity. Marvel of life through agony, and birth through labor.

"How mud-splashed," says Peter Viereck in *The First Morning*, "what a mangy miracle!"—

> Writhes out of owl and stands with drooping wing.
> Just stands there. Moulted, naked, two-thirds dead.
> From shock and pain (and dread of holy dread)
> Suddenly vomiting.
> Look away quick; you are watching the birth of song.

By giving birth, man is born. Only by mediating life is man truly alive.

Selected Bibliography

DHORME, PAUL. *Le livre de Job.* (*"Études bibliques."*) Paris: J. Gabalda, 1926.

DRIVER, S. R., and GRAY, G. B. *A Critical and Exegetical Commentary on the Book of Job.* ("International Critical Commentary.") New York: Charles Scribner's Sons, 1921.

HÖLSCHER, GUSTAV. *Das Buch Hiob.* (*"Handbuch zum Alten Testament."*) Rev. ed. Tubingen: J. C. B. Mohr, 1952.

KISSANE, EDWARD J. *The Book of Job.* Dublin: Browne & Nolan, 1939.

KÖNIG, EDUARD. *Das Buch Hiob.* Gütersloh: C. Bertelsmann, 1929.

KRAELING, EMIL G. *The Book of the Ways of God.* New York: Charles Scribner's Sons, 1939.

PEAKE, A. S. *Job.* ("The Century Bible.") London: T. C. & E. C. Jack, 1904.

STEVENSON, W. B. *The Poem of Job.* London: British Academy, 1947.

————. *Critical Notes on the Hebrew Text of The Poem of Job.* Aberdeen: Aberdeen University Press, 1951.

STRAHAN, JAMES. *The Book of Job.* Edinburgh: T. & T. Clark, 1913.

WATSON, ROBERT ADDISON. *The Book of Job.* ("The Expositor's Bible.") New York: A. C. Armstrong & Son, 1899.

WEISER, ARTUR. *Das Buch Hiob.* Göttingen: Vandenhoeck & Ruprecht, 1951.

Index of Passages

Chapters	Character	Page
3	Job	41
4-5	Eliphaz	69
6-7	Job	52
8	Bildad	79
9-10	Job	103
11	Zophar	84
12-14	Job	118
15	Eliphaz	88
16-17	Job	134
18	Bildad	91
19	Job	142
20	Bildad	92
21	Job	156
22	Eliphaz	94, 96
23-24	Job	160
25-26	Bildad	97
26-27	Job	168
27	Zophar	98
28	Hymn on Wisdom	170
29-31	Job	175
32-37	Elihu	190
38-42	The Lord	219